KEY

To Great Leadership

Rediscovering the Principles of Outstanding Service

Lessons from the front lines of the world's best service companies

PETER BURWASH

TORCHLIGHT PUBLISHING INC.
BADGER, CA, USA
KOLKATA, WEST BENGAL, INDIA

This edition is an updated and revised edition of The Key to Great Leadership, originally published in 1995 by Torchlight Publishing, which was a revised and updated edition of a work titled Who Cares? A Wake Up Call for Service and Leadership, that was previously published and copyrighted by Peter Burwash International in 1993.

Designed by Kurma Rupa dasa
Printed in India

Published simultaneously in the United States of America and
Canada by Torchlight Publishing.

Library of Congress Cataloging-in-Publication Data

Burwash, Peter.
  The key to great leadership : rediscovering the principles of outstanding service lessons from the front lines of the world's best service companies / by Peter Burwash. – Rev. ed.

      p.   cm.
   ISBN 10: 0-9779785-0-8
   ISBN 13: 978-09779785-0-5
      1. Service industries–Management. 2. Service industries–Customer services. 3. Leadership. I. Title.
   HD9980.5.B82 2006
   658.8'12–dc22   2006011879

Attention Colleges, Universities, Corporations, Associations, and Professional Organizations: The Key to Great Leadership is available at special discounts for bulk purchases for training, sales promotions, premiums, fund-raising, or educational use. Special books, booklets, or excerpts can be created to suit your specific needs. For information, contact the publisher.

Torchlight Publishing Inc,.PO Box 52, Badger CA 93603, USA
www.torchlight.com

Dedication

This book is dedicated to my Mom, who taught me to say thank you, and to my Dad, who personified humility.

Acknowledgments

My sincere thanks to all those who generously shared their time and wisdom with me during our interviews. Their names are too numerous to mention, but their thoughts formulated this book.

A special thank you to Gloria South, Chris Dyer, Karen Kruse, Craig O'Shannessy, John Reade, Tom Dyer, Suzie Hodges, Paul Groover, Jean Greisser, Roy Richard, Stewart Cannon, Marie Shaft, Victoria Taylor, Sharon Digby, Craig Escalante, and George Foster for their efforts in helping to put this book together; and to Alister Taylor, my publisher, who is a true professional whose work ethic and personal concern made it happen.

"*Peter Burwash has it right. Total commitment to high value customer service creates long-term success.*"

Ron Allen, former Chairman
Delta Airlines

"*If something is not going right,* The Key *will impact your thinking on all elements of leadership. Its reminders are the ingredients of leading.*"

Peter Ueberroth, Time magazine's
Man of the Year

"The Key to Great Leadership *is one of the most practical and commonsensical approaches to quality service that I have had the pleasure to read.*"

Lawrence M. Johnson, former Chairman
and CEO, Bancorp Hawaii, Inc.
and Bank of Hawaii

"*You have hit the nail on the head with your insights on service…an outstanding book.*"

Fred S. Olmstead,
Federal Express Corporation

"Drawing on his leadership experience, the author spotlights and enlivens the spectrum of factors that make for better leadership."

Robert Galvin, Sr., Chairman of the
Executive Committee, Motorola

"Short, fast-paced and very helpful in comparing our management characteristics."

Bruce Karatz, Chairman
and CEO, Kaufman Broad

"Creating a high-performance, self-disciplined, service-oriented workforce is now the make-or-break function of business leadership, and in his book Peter Burwash, having made his own company a leader by rigorously practicing what he preaches, tells us clearly and concisely how it's done."

Isadore Sharp, Founder and Chairman
of Four Seasons Hotels and Resorts

"Peter's review of effective leaders is appropriate both in theme and substance. He strikes a responsive chord with everyone."

Tom Bolman, Executive Director,
International Association of
Conference Centers

"The Key is so much on target—we use it as a constant reminder on how to upgrade our service and, more importantly, improve on our chances of success."

Jim Baugh, President
Tennis Industry Association

"My cabinet and senior staff were simply overwhelmed by your excellent presentation. . ."

Mufi Hannemann, Mayor, City of Honolulu

Contents

Part One

The 12 Universal Principles of Great Service Companies

Foreword

There has never been a better time to stress the link between leadership and service. We have entered a new economy, increasingly dominated by service. The service sector now provides almost four-fifths of all jobs in the U.S., making it our largest job provider, our major producer of wealth and our only hope for continued economic growth. But unless we can raise the average service worker's output and income, our overall standard of living will inevitably decline, the gap between rich and poor will widen and the social fabric will unravel.

Raising service productivity is our greatest management challenge. It is also a matter of social conscience, as well as an imperative of corporate survival—and it holds profound implications for how we manage. Old-style command-and-control doesn't work in the new service economy. Service is redefining management as leadership.

Peter Burwash is one of the pacemakers in this new service economy. He was a teenage tennis teacher at a club in Toronto when he gave me my first tennis lesson 30-odd years ago. He impressed me, not just as a natural athlete, but as a born teacher, highly sensitive to others and instinctively skilled in responding.

After a near-crippling injury in big-league hockey, he came back to tennis as a fledgling pro to take one of the toughest survival tests in the game: five months on the European tennis circuit. We talked on his return. He was flat broke. But he still wanted to see if he had what it took to be a winner.

Two friends and I put up $3500 to back Peter, who went on to win the Canadian Open and 19 international titles. In 1975, he founded Peter Burwash International (PBI), which now supplies tennis teachers to clubs and resorts in 34 countries, including some of our hotels. I'm not sure it's true, as Peter maintains, that he owes his career to our backing, but I'm certain that $3500 was never invested better.

Peter has made his firm the biggest and best of its kind in the world by following the precepts he outlines in *The Key*. He knows that the first task of a leader is to decide where his company is going and how to get there—and to make sure every employee knows it too and follows through. He knows how to create a high-trust culture and a high-energy work force. In the pages that follow, he tells you—concisely and clearly, from experience rather than scholarship alone—exactly how it's done.

Isadore Sharp,
Founder and Chairman,
Four Seasons Hotels and Resorts

Introduction

The President of the United States, the CEO of a Fortune 500 company, and the mother of an eight-year-old Cub Scout are all in positions of leadership. Those positions share certain common principles, perhaps the most important of which is the fact that good leadership comes through good service. All great service companies in the world also have something in common—they encourage all their members to be leaders. The connection between good leadership and good service is undeniable.

However, there seems to be a disheartening decrease of good service around the world. Many people overlook the simple truth that both economically and on a higher, personal level, we can do the most good for ourselves by doing good to others.

According to a study conducted by The Forum Corporation, an international training and consulting firm, seventy percent of those customers who change companies do so because of poor service. Even more disturbing is the fact that of those who change, 96% do so without a word to the company they left. These figures represent a tremendous, unnecessary loss of potential business. If those companies had adequate service, their customers would never have gone elsewhere in search of better service.

Probably few people on the face of the Earth understand the importance of good service—and its connection to effective leadership—better than Peter Burwash. He has traveled the equivalent of more than 400 times around the equator over the last 30 years, visiting over 130 countries with a multitude of different cultures, and has been exposed to practically every level of service known to man. Tennis champion, keynote speaker, best-selling author and successful entrepreneur, Peter Burwash is the founder and president of one of the highest-rated service companies in the world today—Peter Burwash International, or PBI.

Recognized by James O'Toole, author of Vanguard Management, as one of the top-ten best-managed service companies around the globe, PBI provides tennis resorts with qualified professional tennis instructors. PBI was one of 17 tennis service companies in the world in 1975. Of those 17, PBI is the only one still actively

in the service industry. With 110 professionals working in over 65 top tennis resorts in 34
countries, PBI is a leader in its field.

A man who lives by his ideals, Peter Burwash
believes in himself, in his goals and, ultimately,
in a Higher Power. If you speak to any of his as-
sociates, they will paint you a picture of a man
who deeply cares about others—who is honest,
enthusiastic, consistent and, above all, committed. Not afraid to make mistakes, Peter does his
best, learns from his errors, and goes on.

Tennis Industry Magazine describes Peter as a
man who "changed the game" of tennis, identi-
fying him as "one of the most influential tennis
teachers of the past two decades." Known as the
"Flying Canadian" in professional tennis circles,
Peter has made his mark on the tennis world by
playing with a passion rarely seen. He doesn't

stop to think about whether he'll be hurt when he dives after a speeding tennis ball. He uses the same enthusiasm and determination that helped him become a tennis champion of the highest caliber to make his own life work—both personally and in the business world.

The Key to Great Leadership is a fast and enjoyable read. It is concise and to the point. Based on information gleaned from thousands of interviews with employees and managers of the world's greatest service organizations, this book is built "from the ground up." Well-chosen anecdotes make the ideas herein lucid and easy to grasp. You will find *The Key to Great Leadership* full of information on how to enrich your life as a leader, whether you're a Chairman of the Board or a parent of three.

The Publishers

Part One

THE 12 UNIVERSAL PRINCIPLES OF GREAT SERVICE COMPANIES

As we moved into the 1990s, it was interesting to see how corporations became increasingly aware of the fact that it was a lot cheaper to keep a customer than to spend more money on advertising to gain a new one. If you treat customers well, they will return.

In the late '60s, I stopped off in Hawaii on my way to play the tennis circuit in New Zealand and Australia. Like many tourists, I rented a car to drive around the island. The car did not have gas in it, so I visited a gas station called McCully's Service Station. What impressed me first was that the two employees came running out to the car. The only other time I have seen that was in the fiction movie Back to the Future. Secondly, when they got to the car, they asked me my name. I was so shocked that I, in turn, asked them their names, along with a few other questions. I learned that Ed and Linell were part of the family business.

After they enthusiastically checked the oil, washed the windows and filled the gas tank, I left on my trip around the island. You can guess where I returned for gas—for the next 18 years. I moved to Hawaii permanently in 1973 and stayed with this gas station until the block on which the station stood was sold. Out of interest I went back through my receipts and found that I had spent through the years $19,217.00 at this particular gas station. During this entire time, they provided their service enthusiastically and promptly.

Loyalty is a very strong factor in people's lives. We like to return to places where we are recognized with enthusiasm, knowing that we will get the best service. I became so loyal to the McCully Service Station that when they finally closed their doors, I honestly didn't know where another gas station was on the island.

We all have a similar story, whether it is our favorite restaurant or shoe repair. The important thing to realize is that our loyalty is almost always based on good service.

Mohandas Karamachand [Mahatma] Gandhi, who inspired such deep loyalty among the diverse people of revolutionary-era India, stated: "The true meaning of life is service."

As we examine the 12 universal principles of the great service companies, I would encourage you to not only evaluate your company yourself-take these principles and ask fellow workers for their evaluation of the company's performance in each of these areas. If your company can score a 9 or a 10 out of 10 in each of these categories, you will be guaranteed success.

Lateral Service

Patron at restaurant:
"Waiter, what time is it?"
Waiter: "Sorry, that's not my table."

The best service companies have a very simple philosophy. They do whatever is necessary to ensure that their customers have an excellent experience and are served beyond their expectations. One of the concepts that helps make this happen is that of "lateral service," where serving fellow employees is given as much importance and emphasis as serving the customer.

Lateral service is often known as esprit de corps or teamwork. It can range from helping out a fellow employee in trouble to doing someone else's job to ensure it gets done. Or as the late Dick Holtzman Sr., a highly regarded hotelier, said, "Lateral service is often the art of making good on somebody else's mistakes." And it translates into a much better experience for the customer.

I witnessed a classic example of lateral service one evening at the Regent of Hong Kong, for many years listed as one of the top hotels in the world. On this particular night there were a lot of arrivals at once. One of the customers in front of me had just flown in from New York and was irate. The lobby is one of the most magnificent of any hotel in the world. Sound carries very well in it, as the original purpose of having such good acoustics was that the piano player on the second floor could be heard upon check-in. On this particular evening the not-so-gentle man from New York was drowning out the piano player with his verbal bashing of a Regent employee.

Even though it was busy, other employees in the lobby suddenly began to surround the customer to see what the problem was and how they might help. Within no time there were eleven employees around him. The effect was dramatic—the gentleman calmed down and started speaking in a civil manner, enabling the staff to help him. I thought at first what might be going through his mind was that he was in a strange city surrounded by eleven strangers and maybe he should behave himself. But the concern for his situation seemed so genuine that he obviously felt that he was the recipient of exceptional interest and service. And the be-

leaguered employee had also been the recipient of service—lateral service. By coming to his
rescue, his fellow employees had assisted him
as well as the customer.

It seems that most hotels, particularly in North
America, are designed with an "escape door"
behind the front desk, which is built conve-
niently for a quick exit. Have you ever noticed
what generally happens when an agitated guest
is giving his sermon to a front desk employee
on how this is the last time he will ever stay at
the hotel? As the abuse becomes greater, the
rest of the employees disappear through the escape hatch or get very busy on their computers.
I have rarely seen an employee come to the rescue of another employee in any business, anywhere in North America. Either some employees like it when another employee is in trouble,

believing it makes them look better in the eyes of their supervisor, or they are just too steeped in the philosophy that "it's not my job."

Lateral service is the direct opposite of saying "it's not my job." It is a willingness to occasionally do another employee's task, which results in better service to the customer. I experienced a prime example of "it's not my job" at the Waldorf Astoria in New York. Because of the history of the place and my fascination with entrepreneurs like Conrad Hilton, I have always enjoyed staying at this hotel. I must add that I normally receive excellent service there. However, one morning when I was checking out, my bags had not come down. After 20 minutes I asked the doorman if he could find out what the problem was. His answer was: "No way. I only go in there once a week to get my paycheck." I couldn't help but feel Conrad Hilton would not have been pleased.

Although unions have provided a valuable service in certain areas, the greatest disservice they have done is to departmentalize people's jobs. Crossover training (having employees learn to do more than one job) is very beneficial. It offers the employee variety and the opportunity to grow and be challenged, rather than being buttonholed into one area. And it enables customers to get better service.

Two years into the research for this book I started doing seminars and speaking engagements on the subject of service. This afforded me the opportunity to share my findings and get feedback for the book. It also afforded a tremendous opportunity to hear new stories and meet new individuals who could help with the book. One of the engagements was for Ritz-Carlton and in the room was then Vice President Horst Schulze (now President). He shared with me a story of an employee willing to do more than just "his job."

One evening a woman stepped out of her room at a Ritz-Carlton hotel and asked the electrician who was working in the room across from her where the ice machine was. In most hotels the employees "point," but it is Ritz-Carlton's philosophy to "escort...not point." The electrician, in a very polite manner, said, "I will get the ice for you ma'am." The woman was impressed enough to write Horst, and this story became part of the Ritz-Carlton culture.

It was interesting to me during the research that a lot of successful leaders had a strong sports background. They understood the need and value of teamwork. Vince Lombardi, the legendary coach of the great 1960s Green Bay Packers football team, constantly stressed that "The whole can be far greater than the sum of the parts." Lombardi also talked a lot about taking care of your fellow teammates.

Over the years I have watched a lot of sports teams practice, but the time with the San Francisco 49ers during the Joe Montana era in the 80s and 90s stands out as the best because it was so impressive to hear the many words of encouragement that were passed between fellow players.

So many people today talk about the breakdown of the American family, yet there's little talk about the breakdown of the extended family. In today's frenetic pace, parents often say they can't get enough proper rest or rejuvenation, especially when caring for young children.

However, work has almost always been an integral part of any society and this problem was solved with the extended family: aunts, uncles, cousins, grandmothers and a network of relatives available to help one another.

Stressing lateral service in an organization or a family results in real teamwork, with everyone knowing they will support each other in doing what is necessary to get the job done. It therefore results in exceptional service.

How is the lateral service concept in your company?

Empowerment

"I will have to ask my supervisor."

A few years ago, motivational and business speakers started encouraging a change in the way we diagrammed the corporate structure on paper. So often, the president, CEO or chairman would be listed at the top. Going down through the levels of management and employees made the chart look like a triangle. Then the idea became popular that this triangle should be turned upside down with the leader of the company at the bottom and the "front-line" employees at the top. By putting those employees at the top of this "reverse triangle," an organization is illustrating their importance to the company. At the very top of this triangle is the customer, whose own feeling of empowerment ultimately determines the success of every transaction. Some companies finally realized the most important people in the company were those who had direct personal contact with the customer.

It is also a way of recognizing that their information and ideas are important and will flow "down" through the organization, giving the employee the power to make a valuable contribution to the company.

The concept of "empowerment" takes this power one step further. It became such a buzzword in the late '80s that I was almost reluctant to use it in this book. However, it perfectly illustrates this concept. It means that employees are "empowered" to make decisions at their level and do not constantly have to go to their boss or supervisor for approval. For example, if a guest checking out of a hotel has a problem with some phone calls on his bill that he did not make, the cashier could make the decision to take them off the bill. The cashier has the "power" to do so without checking with his supervisor. If the front desk clerk has to say, "Let me check with my supervisor," you know empowerment is not part of the hotel's culture.

Empowerment is often a difficult concept for top management who have been used to making all the decisions or who like to micro-manage. However, as wise decisions are made by knowledgeable employees throughout all levels, top executives are freed up to plan for the future and to be creative. This concept has been hardest on middle managers because their role has suddenly changed from giving orders to coaching.

An important point must be made here. It is CRITICAL that managers back up the decision of the employee, EVEN IF IT IS WRONG. If a poor decision is made, the manager's position is to explain how things might be done differently next time—without showing any anger or disappointment.

Training employees is obviously very important in order for the concept of empowerment to work successfully within an organization. When workers are making decisions affecting the financial viability of the enterprise, they must understand the philosophy and policies of the company and be trained to deal with whatever arises.

If an employee understands the company's philosophy in doing business, and receives good training, there is no need to detail what needs to be done in every circumstance. The company shows trust and confidence that employees will make the appropriate decisions and actions, and the employees tend to live up to that expectation.

Ritz-Carlton Hotels won the Malcolm Baldrige National Quality Award, which honors companies that have superior products or services and an ongoing quality-improvement program. Ritz-Carlton managers say the most important thing they do is to give employees the power to deliver quality and service at every turn. Without checking with a supervisor, a front-desk clerk can alter a bill if there is a problem, or a housekeeper can order a new washing machine if she feels it is needed. Executives are very involved in the monitoring and training of employees to provide service and every employee receives more than 100 hours a year in quality training.

Federal Express (also a Malcolm Baldrige winner) has been consistently cited as another company that successfully uses the concept of empowerment. Employees know they can exercise their own judgment in making decisions to ensure customer satisfaction. Almost everyone who has dealt with Federal Express has a story about an employee who went out of his or her way to make sure a package reached its destination on time. Probably the most famous (and most expensive) example is that of the Federal Express employee who chartered a helicopter to get a small package to a customer after the package could not be delivered due to a snow storm. Obviously decisions such as this cannot be repeated on a regular basis, as the financial viability of a company would be in jeopardy; however, it is a classic example of Federal Express' structure and their understanding of empowerment.

Jan Carlzon, former Chairman of Scandinavian Airlines Systems (SAS), dramatically turned around the company in 1981 by empowering his employees. In his book, Moments of Truth, Carlzon talked a lot about empowerment as an opportunity to win the loyalty of the customer. He stressed the fact that people are impressed when they are dealing with a company of leaders and decision makers, regardless of their titles.

Another very powerful example of empowerment occurred at the Marriott Hotel in Hong Kong. A banker, his wife and young child came into the restaurant for lunch. All the highchairs for young children were in use, so the waiter, having received the course in empowerment, immediately went downstairs to a shopping mall and bought an extra highchair. Is it any wonder that that gentleman is a Marriott customer for life?

If your company does not score highly in the area of empowerment, a change is needed. Remember, customers don't like to hear, "I'll have to check with my supervisor."

Visible Leaders

*"In the best companies, employees see
their leader every day."*
DICK HOLTZMAN, SR.

When reading Tom Peters' and Bob Waterman's book *In Search of Excellence* (the first of the multitude of books on modern business), I found the most relevant point was their MBWA philosophy. This stood for "Management By Wandering Around." For some reason, as we moved into the productive era of the '60s and '70s, it became harder to find and see the leaders and managers. Even today in the 21st century, have you ever noticed how difficult it is to find the executive offices in hotels or department stores? When was the last time you had a general manager help check you into a hotel, unless you happen to be a VIP? Or better still, when was the last time you had a general manager say goodbye to you or talk to you in line as you stood waiting, as customer number 16, to give the hotel your money? I truly believe that if more managers were there at check-out, they would learn more about their hotels than at any other time. Guest comment cards are one thing, but face-to-face interaction with a customer who is waiting in line to pay the bill at 6:00 a.m. will probably give a more accurate feel of what they thought of their stay.

More importantly, great service companies need a manager or leader who will wander around for the benefit of the employees. Visible leaders show by their actions that they are involved. My MBWA award over the years goes to Felix Bieger, former General Manager at the Peninsula Hotel in Hong Kong. He was constantly roaming the hotel, trying to ensure that the facilities, the service and the experience were the best they could be. He was very accessible to guests and employees, and both benefited from his presence. The Peninsula, under his leadership, was always considered one of the premier hotels in the world.

Another notable example was on the Crystal Cruises' ship, Symphony. The hotel manager had a glass door—you could see whether or not he was at his desk (no assistant, no secretary, no barricades)—direct access to the leader. Small, but critical details such as this have kept Crystal Cruises the leader in the cruise ship industry.

Obviously, the bigger the company, the tougher it is for leaders to be able to give the necessary time to each and every employee. However, any interaction with a company's leader can be the key in expressing an overall attitude to employees.

When my wife and I were checking into the Four Seasons Newport, the bellman welcomed us to the hotel and asked if we had stayed there before. I told him it was our first time but that we often stayed at Four Seasons Hotels. I added that Issy Sharp (Chairman and founder of Four Seasons) was a good friend of mine and that I grew up with him in Toronto. The bellman very politely replied, "Issy Sharp is a good friend of mine also." Now I am sure if I asked Issy about their relationship or talked to the bellman further, I would have found that they are probably not friends at the closest level. But what is important is that the bellman truly feels that Issy is his good friend. This is one of the real reasons why Four Seasons is rated as one of the truly finest firms in the world and why many of their individual hotels are on most people's top-ten lists.

At the other end of the spectrum, there was a hotel in San Diego that had a prominent international company managing it. As I was evaluating the hotel and meeting with management and employees, I spent some time with a front desk clerk at a particularly slow time. I asked this young lady what she thought of her general manager. She said, "I don't know. I haven't met him." To which I responded, "How long have you been working here?" When she replied six months, it became clear why the employee turnover rate at that hotel was 300%.

With the big hotel chains comes the potential

danger that the general manager becomes a "desk jockey." The original hotelier was ever visible. However, with big hotel chains, the headquarters office often requires a good deal of paperwork. This is very unfortunate, as most people come into the hotel business not to push paper but, rather, to greet customers and be a host or hostess. As I interviewed general managers of the hospitality industry worldwide, their number one frustration was that corporate headquarters did not allow them to do what they really wanted to do—take care of the customers. Personally, I think this is one of the biggest mistakes in this modern era of the service industry. There are many enthusiastic, hospitable general managers who hardly ever get to see their customers, and it has hurt the industry in terms of a quality guest experience.

As a sideline to our story about the hotel in San

Diego, I found out that the general manager did not like to interact with people and did not really care about his employees. Is it any surprise that the owners of the hotel broke the contract early and switched management firms?

An obvious benefit of getting a chance to update and revise a book comes after you meet people who have read the book. In November 1997, I was at the Homestead Resort having breakfast with its then President, Gary Rosenberg. Gary related the following story. One night he was lying in the bathtub at 10:00 p.m., reading this book prior to going to bed. He got so excited reading the section about wandering around that he got dressed to just walk around, talking to employees. He recalled a special moment where he sat down with one of the employees that he had never got to spend much time with

prior to this. They had a very inspiring conversation. The gentleman had a heart attack
shortly thereafter. Gary was very thankful that
he had made the decision to give up some sleep
time to spend with this individual. Anyone who
has been to the Homestead recently can attest
to the fact that there is a heartbeat back in the
hotel.

How does your corporate leader rate in terms
of visibility?

Statement of
Commitment to Service

*"We are ladies and gentlemen
serving ladies and gentlemen."*
RITZ-CARLTON CREDO

Of all the people I interviewed for this book, perhaps the most passionate about service was former President of Ritz-Carlton Hotel Company, Horst Schulze. Horst talked about service with fire in his eyes: "Most hotels are in the shelter industry, but we at Ritz-Carlton are in the service industry."

The credo above, that all Ritz-Carlton employees carry with them, is wonderfully simple and
practical. This statement of commitment relays
the dignity of their position and enables employees to feel good about themselves, while understanding their role in the service industry.

Jan Carlzon, when President of SAS, changed
that airline, from an 80 million dollar a year
loser in the late '70s, into a very profitable business a few years later. When asked how this happened, he stated simply, "In 1981 we stopped
flying aircraft and started serving customers."

One of the biggest turnarounds in terms of attitude toward customer service came in the early
1990s, when British Airways started to look at
the customer as being someone who might be
somewhat valuable to their future. I remember
getting off the plane on two different flights and

having someone interview me as to my thoughts on the overall experience. In all my years of traveling, this was the only time I had ever been interviewed after a flight and thousands of other flyers were surveyed as well. The end result is British Airways' transition from a very impersonal airline to one that now has a strong customer service attitude and a solid product that the customer wants and it has shown in the bottom line. One of the reasons that you seldom see any of the American carriers in the top-20 rating in the world is because there is very little time spent talking to the people who actually sit in the seats. The general philosophy of the American air carriers seems to be "what less can we do for you?"

As I traveled around the world interviewing management and employees, it became very evident that there were few corporations or business entities that had a true statement of commitment to service. A company's commitment to service is reflected in the words and actions of its employees. In 1988 I experienced an interesting example of this in the contrasting attitudes of two pilots, one at Eastern and one at Delta.

I did not enjoy the Los Angeles to Atlanta "Red-eye Flight" which leaves L.A. at 10 p.m. and gets into Atlanta around 5:00 a.m, but had I not taken this trip twice in one week I could not share this story with you. As many frequent flyers may recall, in the mid-1980s pilots started to open their cockpit door upon arrival and thank their customers for flying with them. And so it was on a Delta flight, standing at the doorway waiting for the airplane door to open, when I felt it was an appropriate time to elicit the pilot's thoughts. With an expression I hoped would show concern, I said, "You sure have a lousy job, having to fly all night and get in at this horrible hour."

In a polite upbeat tone he replied, "No sir, we are in the business of serving customers. And besides, aircraft do not make money sitting on the ground." When I told this story to then Chairman of Delta, Ron Allen, during our interview, he was delighted because it brought out two things. First of all, the pilot understood the real reason for flying, namely to serve the customer. Secondly, he understood the economics, namely that aircraft truly are financially unproductive sitting on the ground.

A few days later I flew the identical route, this time on Eastern. Once again I was first in line to get off the aircraft, and with the same expression I made the same statement to the Eastern pilot, "You sure have a lousy job, having to fly all night and get in at this horrible hour." The Eastern pilot bitched until the door opened. A few years later Eastern filed for bankruptcy and Delta became one of the world's mega-carriers. Perhaps it goes back to Eastern's culture. I was told that the founder of Eastern Airlines, Eddie Rickenbacher, used to tell customers, "You are damn lucky to fly my airline." Even though Eastern had a lot of wonderful human beings as employees, the overall culture and understanding of a true commitment to service was never able to filter throughout the company.

What is sad, though, is that Delta in 2004 lost more money than any carrier in the history of aviation. In the mid-'90s, I felt the rapid decline of Delta's commitment to service. I went from a frequent Delta flyer to flying them only when there was no alternative. More on this demise in Chapter 6.

How is your company's statement of commitment to service?

Hiring the Attitude, then Training

*"You are only as good as the
the people you hire."*

Good corporations look for people who have an attitude of sincerely wanting to help people. This caring service approach comes from within and is not something you can teach through training programs or Policy and Procedure manuals. Real service is not thought of as a sacrifice, and it transcends a paycheck.

It has been my general observation that in the Western world we tend to be more selfish than service-oriented. In most of the Asian countries, taking care of people is programmed from childhood. It is part of the culture that the younger folks take care of their elders. If the attitude is not naturally there—even if service is stressed—it is hard to avoid what I call "formula courtesy," namely, a cardboard thank you and plastic smile.

Even though Singapore Airlines continues to be ranked the number one airline in the world, a lot of their senior management have been concerned about the fact that their employees were perceived as "robots" who did not personalize the service at the level the customer wanted. Employees were often locked into certain phrases and answers that were to be given, and this took away from their individual personalities. What is impressive is that even though Singapore Airlines is number one, they continue to listen to the customer regularly and are willing to grow and change.

What makes a great company is the sincerity, genuine friendliness, and attitude of the employees—and this has to be throughout the company. Almost everyone has experienced a great tasting meal being ruined when it's served by a rude waiter or waitress.

Something that human resource people throughout the world need to look at as well is whether or not an individual is willing to do all the menial tasks that are necessary to ensure that the customer's needs and wants are taken care of. In over thirty years of travel what has amazed me is the fact that at the end of a ten-hour flight on an American carrier, the washrooms are pretty much "trashed out." Yet the Asian carriers, for the most part, are as immaculate in the tenth hour as they were at the beginning of the flight. When I made calls to ask the American carriers why this was the case, the comment was that "We have trouble getting our flight attendants to see it as their responsibility to take care of the washrooms." Call this an error in hiring or an overzealous set of union rules or poor leadership, but the bottom line is that this attitude has to change.

Hiring someone who does not have a service attitude, and then trying to train them in it, is a little like the expression, "You can't teach a pig to sing; it just wastes your time and annoys the pig." The best companies seek out and find people who see it as an honor to be able to serve others.

The brightest new star in the service business
this last decade has to go to Crystal Cruises.
What was so impressive about the entire staff
was the consistency of their attitude toward
service. Every section of their ship, The Crystal
Harmony, had people willing to help the customer have a great experience.

And they did it without any hint of incon-
venience. In most service businesses, only a
small minority display an outstanding attitude
throughout their staff. From the veteran to the
new hire, the attitudes of the Crystal employees
were exemplary.

What's their secret? Perhaps the guest on board
said it the best, "They hire very few Americans."
On a five-star cruise ship there are numerous
jobs, both in the areas of safety and hospitality;
and though Americans are very enthusiastic,

they generally are not enthused doing tasks perceived as menial. I have often felt that the ideal employee would be a mix of many cultures; but if I had to pick three, it would be the enthusiasm of the average American, the attention to detail of the average Japanese, and the warmth and humility of the average Thai.

How has your company done in terms of hiring attitude first?

Encouraging Participation,
or a Sense of Family

*"The firefighter holding the ladder is
as important as the firefighter
holding the hose."*

In updating this book, I was inclined to eliminate the following story, but it is still a great example of what made a company once wonderful to work with.

Those involved in the hospitality industry are still amazed that, in the '80s, Delta Airline employees purchased an entire aircraft for the company to say thank you. Delta's sense of family had been evident. Through the years they had made every effort to avoid laying off their employees. Even though in times of crisis pilots have had to handle baggage, they still received a paycheck. Good families are loyal to all of their family members, and Delta exhibited this as well as anyone.

When I interviewed Ron Allen, then President of Delta, what fascinated me most were the number of stories he told that brought home Delta's sense of family. Ron's eyes lit up each time he told a story demonstrating how he encouraged participation among the Delta family. One of his favorites occurred shortly after Delta started to fly internationally. Flight attendants were telling him that the aircraft was not designed appropriately for international flights.

He subsequently got flight attendants together with the engineers to help design the new aircraft.

Such participation seems so practical, yet as I interviewed employees at many companies, it became clear that this simply does not happen enough. Employees believe they have the knowledge, the understanding and, in most cases, the answers. But they can't get management to listen. The frustration is eating them up.

All of the above occurred prior to the 1990s, when Delta went into a major expansion. There's a lot of speculation as to what subsequently happened, but within a very short space of time Delta was no longer the friendly carrier it once was. It had become very impersonal, and now employees were talking negatively about management and the company. By 1997, it was easy to engage a Delta employee in a conversation about what was wrong with the company. The Delta family had started to break apart quickly.

Perhaps our most blatant misuse, or rather "non-use," of knowledge occurs in the restaurant business. Whenever you ask who made up the menu, it is usually the chef, the maitre d' and/or the manager. Yet who has the most customer contact? The waiters and waitresses. In only the rarest of circumstances do they participate in helping to make up the menu. I doubt there has ever been a day in a restaurant when a waitress did not get a special request to do up something different from what was on the menu. Yet in today's fast-paced era, there is so little contact between waiters and waitresses and the chef and manager, that valuable information is seldom exchanged. Managers complain about the high turnover rates with waiters and waitresses, but would you want to stay in a job if all you were asked to do was carry food from the kitchen to the table, with little opportunity to use your brain cells?

The staff of the Marriott at Chicago O'Hare Airport found that on average more than 70 irons per evening were being requested. They suggested to management that it might be a good idea to have irons in all of the rooms, as a lot of manpower was being used each evening. Wouldn't it be a great investment in the long run? All 1200 rooms now have irons.

Surprisingly, many automobiles today have been designed without the input of mechanics, the individuals who ultimately have to service the car. Saturn Corporation, the so-called renegade car company and off-shoot of General Motors, has a great policy. Employees sit in on the design planning of the car. Their approach is very important: "Involvement of the individual as a member of a team is the definitive move that companies must make in the future. Organizations will win as teams. The job of manager is to function as a team, not as an individual. When companies realize this, it is awesome."

Almost everybody knows what are at the top of employees' wish-lists, namely recognition and appreciation. But not a lot are aware of the third—creative freedom.

This also applies cross-culturally. Even when I interview Japanese employees, this is something they want most.

Getting employees involved at all levels and giving them a sense of family and participation will not only have a major impact on employee turn-over, but also on the bottom line.

Does your company encourage this kind of engaging participation?

Sense of Urgency

*"You cannot build a reputation
on what you are going to do."*
HENRY FORD

I read an article a few years ago that stated
only 2% of the American population has a true
sense of urgency. Although I couldn't help but
wonder if the exact figure wasn't somewhat ex-
aggerated, there was an essential truth in the article. I remember it well, as I had just returned
from a Sony repair shop in Honolulu, Hawaii,
where this certainly proved true. I dictate an average of 1400 letters a month (slightly less now

with email), but these dictating machines are still very important business allies. Here is what transpired after I had stood in line for twenty minutes:

I said to the gentleman behind the counter: "This machine is very important to me and I would appreciate it if I could get it repaired as soon as possible."

Sony employee: "Six weeks."

My response: "Pardon me?"

Sony employee: "Six weeks, minimum."

My next response: "But I need this urgently. Can I pay extra?"

Sony employee: "I said six weeks. That's the best we can do."

I reluctantly left the machines, but on the drive home I mentally prepared a fax to Aki Morita, then Chairman of Sony. Aki was a big proponent of service and I know that he would have been horrified had he witnessed this conversation. It is interesting to note that within hours of my sending the fax, I received a call from Sony's repair center, telling me the machines would be ready first thing in the morning.

Why is it that Nordstrom's, a department store famous for its service, has a one-day tailoring service when most others are seven to ten days? It is simply because Nordstrom's makes a sense of urgency part of their service culture. Others could, too.

In 1988, under the astute leadership of then Chairman of the Board Bob Galvin Sr., Motorola won the Malcolm Baldrige Award for quality and service in American business. One of the biggest steps Motorola took in upgrading their service to customers was cutting the time between the receipt of a customer order and shipment of a product from two months to two hours. This type of dramatic change can be done in any company.

The best example in today's computer era is Dell Computers. Michael Dell truly understands the essence of urgency, and it is this urgency to fill a customer's needs that has been a major pillar of the company's success.

Is it any wonder that the number one customer complaint about most service enterprises is long lines? The number two customer complaint is that when lines get long, nearby employees pretend not to notice.

Employees should be like white corpuscles in the blood stream—they should rush to wherever help is needed. If there are long lines, employees should rush to take care of that problem. NOBODY enjoys standing in line.

I noted with interest that Japanese car makers in the late '80s began to allow their customers to come into their offices and select the car they wanted on Monday; it would be built to their specifications for pick-up by Friday. Lately, they are striving to have delivery by Wednesday.

How does your company stack up in terms of a sense of urgency?

True Concern for
the Customer

*"There's only one boss: the customer.
He can fire anybody by spending
money elsewhere."*

SAM WALTON

In over 30 years of being on the road 200-250
days each year, the most pleasant time for me
to travel was during mid-January to the end of
February in 1991—the Gulf War. Every customer was treated like royalty, because there were
so few people traveling. It was the only time I

can recall being consistently respected as a traveler. People had big smiles on their faces when you came up to the counter. They truly appreciated your business and let you know it. If only it didn't take something so drastic to get companies to treat their customers with the utmost respect. The same scenario might have happened after September 11th except for the fact that the airlines cut out so many flights and people were so paranoid checking out all the passengers who might be suspicious.

I have often wondered how many businesses are actually able to stay alive as long as they do. I am sure that if people were not prone to accidents and somewhat negligent in the way they take care of their health, hospitals would be among the first places to go out of business. If you have ever been to an emergency room, you've seen what happens when someone comes in, obviously suffering and in pain. They can barely sit or stand up, yet must fill in a long and complicated form and then have a seat, often for hours. The attitude that can come across in hospitals is that they are doing us a favor, even though we may literally have to empty our pockets for their services. Since good health is paramount, I am shocked at the incredible lack of concern for the customer (patient) in most hospitals or doctor's offices.

I live in Carmel Valley in Northern California. The climate is wonderful and I decided to start a garden for the first time in my life. In getting rid of the weeds, I developed a rash. It took four months to get an appointment with a doctor who specialized in skin care. In the first visit, the doctor carved out tissue for testing. During the next three sessions at his office, he said he did not know what it was, yet charged me $140.00 for each visit (not covered by insurance). On the fourth trip I planned to confront him about this, but he had me sitting there for over an hour on this visit before he could see me. I had to pick up my daughter from karate and I just walked out. The receptionist was unfazed by my telling her that I was leaving. I never heard from that doctor again. There was no follow-up on his part. I wish all rashes were instantly eradicated and this doctor would be on the street begging for help.

In today's computer world we have an opportunity to let our customers know that we do appreciate them. A number of years ago I was having dinner with Rudy Greiner, then General Manager of the Regent of Hong Kong, and he asked me what my favorite drink was. I replied that my favorite drink was carrot juice. About six months later I returned to the Regent of Hong

Kong as a guest and in my room's refrigerator was a large jug of carrot juice. For 10 years now whenever I have stayed at the hotel, the carrot juice is waiting. On one of my more recent trips, just before landing at Hong Kong's Kai Tak Airport, I found my mouth watering over the thought of the carrot juice that would be waiting in the hotel. Although the room rates have more than quadrupled during that time, I still stay there because of the carrot juice. In fact at one point we were thinking of calling this book *In Search of Carrot Juice* because the story exemplified so much the point of really caring about customers and their individual needs.

It is very important that companies let their customers know their business is truly appreciated. Often customers spend a lot of money and companies don't even have the courtesy to write them a thank you letter, or even a few simple words of appreciation.

One of the most important tenets companies can live by is that they should treat every customer as if the success of the business depended on that individual alone. Great service is pleasing customers, one at a time.

Every so often each of us has a story of exceptional service where you, the customer, felt special. For me the place was the lobby of the Four Seasons Singapore Hotel. I had a 6:30 a.m. departure, so I came down to the lobby at 3:30 a.m. Waiting to say goodbye to me was the General Manager, Chris Norton. He was dressed in a three-piece suit and asked me to sit down, and then asked me what I had noticed that could be improved upon in the hotel. We sat down to talk and in front of me was placed my favorite drink, a glass of carrot juice. Here is one of the finest run hotels anywhere in the world and the general manager wants to know how to make it better. Chris Norton is a general manager who truly walks his talk, and his talk is very simple, yet extremely powerful: "There is nothing more noble than to serve."

Since a large part of my life is sitting in aircraft seats, it is an appropriate time to share two personal highlights where companies showed true concern for their customer. First was a flight on Virgin Air. This is one of the most exciting airlines to fly on, headed up by one of my service heroes, Richard Branson from England. I was sitting in an economy seat, which by the way was better than some airlines' business-class seats. From behind the curtain emerged none other than the President and founder of Virgin Air, Richard Branson himself. He was walking up and down the aisle with a notepad talking to customers, trying to find out what they wanted. The end result was a plethora of innovations in the airline industry. By the end of 1997, he was employing over a hundred massage therapists on his flights. There were hair stylists and a separate section for families. Hand-held computers to check in passengers waiting in line. Every few months Virgin announces a new idea, all aimed at enhancing the customer experience. When was the last time you saw the chairman or president of an airline coming back to talk to you, to get YOUR ideas? Sir Richard Branson is perhaps the most innovative, personally concerned business leader of the century.

One other time a few years ago, I got a call from Paul Casey, then Vice President of Continental Airlines International Division. He asked me to help evaluate a new seat they were experimenting with. He said that it was going to be called BusinessFirst. Continental Airlines was coming out of two bankruptcies and they had a tough road ahead, as the airline did not have a good reputation. Yet by the end of 1996, they had been voted the best airline in the U.S. two years in a row, and one of the reasons was the BusinessFirst seat. It is an outstanding product and makes long-haul flying a very bearable exercise. It is interesting to note that this experiment was the start of Continental's rise to viability. Gordon Bethune, its Chairman for a number of years, chronicled this turn-around in a book called From Worst to First.

How is your company in terms of really caring about the customer?

9

High Level of Appreciation for Employees

"If you don't acknowledge efforts, you ultimately get mediocre performances."

Ken Blanchard probably did more in his book *The One Minute Manager* than anyone to bring forth the concept of "catch people doing things right." For some reason many leaders have the mentality that it is their role and duty to catch people doing things wrong. Once this kind of mentality permeates the culture of an organization, the employees become fearful. A sword-wielding leader will never get the best from his employees. People may respond short term to this approach, but in the long term they will move on to another job. I'm amazed at how many leaders still think they have to be Attila the Hun. It is interesting to note, however, that those individuals who manage by fear are usually the most insecure. They dread the thought of any of their employees being able to do a job better than they or assume any leadership role that might usurp their power. Another interesting discovery was that these leaders actually believe their employees enjoy working for them, when in fact the fear they instill simply fosters hate or disgust.

Another segment of leaders, though small, run their enterprises by way of expectation. In other words, they feel that since they give a paycheck to their people every two to four weeks, they can expect a high level of performance. They expect the job will always be done well and therefore appreciation is not necessary. When their employees were interviewed, in almost every instance one of the things that they longed for was appreciation by their boss or leader.

The purpose of a great organization is to make great people, and one of the ways to help make great individuals is to show a deep sense of appreciation. This appreciation should extend into full support for the employees as well. The well-known phrase "the customer is always right" can often put employees in a difficult position, because in fact the customer is NOT always right. There are instances where the customer is definitely wrong, but in order to keep good public relations, an employee must treat the

customer as if he were right. In such instances
it is very important to employees that their boss
lets them know that they acted appropriately
and recognizes that the employees were in fact
right. This way the customer goes away feeling
happy and the employee feels management's
support in what may have been an uncomfortable situation. The way employees treat the
customer reflects the manner they are treated
by management.

I would like to relate a story that illustrates management not showing its appreciation to employees. I was coming into one of the mega-re-
sorts of Hawaii as part of a planning committee
for a conference. One of the employees, Tom,
had recognized my name on the arrival sheet
and did something very special for me. In the
early '70s when I was on the professional tennis
tour, he had been a line judge at tournaments

and had also read a story mentioning I was a vegetarian. Tom remembered this and talked to the chef at this hotel to organize special meals for me each night. I was so impressed by his thoughtfulness and personal concern that I wrote the chairman of the board of the hotel chain, the president, the general manager of the hotel, and Tom's immediate supervisor. Three months later I returned to the resort for another meeting and saw Tom again. I asked him if he had received a copy of my letter from any of the four people involved or if my commendation had been mentioned to him. When he said no, I understood why the turnover of employees at the hotel was so great. And guess what? The hotel filed for bankruptcy a few years later and the general manager never got another job in the hospitality business.

When I would confront a manager or leader as to why they did not show more appreciation to employees, the two common answers were that they didn't have time or they didn't think it was important. Let me say this: If an organization doesn't show a high level of appreciation for employees, it will not be successful. Employees will not stand for it—and they shouldn't.

The ultimate example of lack of appreciation and concern is the abrupt termination of employees who have given 15 to 20 years of their life in good service to a company. Necessity of "cut-backs" is a reality during hard times—but is difficult to accept while company leaders are helping themselves to hefty bonuses and exorbitantly high salaries. Good leaders care about their employees, not just as workers, but as human beings. Loyalty should start from the top; when it does, it permeates through all employees.

Scandinavian Airlines Systems (SAS) has a most progressive headquarters, designed to really serve the employee. Concern is shown in many ways—from the quality of food in the cafeteria to various activities planned for the employees. I also like the design of the SAS headquarters for another reason. There are no signs in the building—the purpose of this is to force inter-action between the employees of the building and guests. This concept has paid off in giving guests a good feeling when they enter the building, because usually an SAS employee will escort them to the appropriate office. People I've talked to who have visited the building had felt the warmth of the reception.

Bob Burns, former Chairman of the Board of Regent International Hotels and one of the industry's outstanding innovators and pioneers of luxury hotels, once had a policy that each employee would stay in the hotel as a guest prior to working at Regent. Not only was this a real pleasure for the employees, but they also got to see and experience what a customer would during his or her time there. It was a great concept that worked.

I can't leave the subject of appreciation without sharing one more story. I was giving a presentation for a company in Hawaii and we were discussing this very point—that management should have a great appreciation for the work done by their employees. As I said this, one of the employees shouted out "Right on, man," and suddenly the room erupted with cheering and clapping. I was aware that management was not that supportive of its employees; however, I was caught totally off-guard by this outburst of anti-management feeling. It took about 30 seconds to get the group quieted down and I realized that I was in an extremely uncomfortable position, as was the management team.

At that point, I asked the employees when they had shown appreciation for the management by either writing them a letter or commending them verbally. It was not surprising that no hands went up. I was then able to expound on the fact that appreciation is a two-way street. Sometimes employees do not understand that a leadership role can be a very lonely one and employees need to show their own appreciation as well. It is not a question of "brown-nosing" the boss, simply a matter of caring enough to say thanks.

Certainly appreciation of management comes more naturally in those companies that demonstrate their sincere concern for employees. We should never forget that appreciation is one of the deepest needs of human nature. It's free, but exceptionally powerful.

Check your meter for the level of appreciation for employees that exists in your company.

10

Extreme Flexibility

*"A tree that bends with
the wind doesn't break."*

When companies or employees are not flexible, what they are actually saying is, "We do
not want your business." When I was trying
to think of a subtitle for this chapter, the one
that came to mind was "The Chef Won't Do It."
Unfortunately, I have had to hear this statement reiterated by many waiters and waitresses
around the world as I attempted to order one of
my former favorite foods, a grilled cheese sand-

wich. Since most of the menus did not include grilled cheese sandwiches, but did have ham and cheese, I always politely asked if they could just leave off the ham. In far too many instances I was told that "the chef won't do it." It is amazing that the managers of these establishments have never been able to educate the chefs to understand that it is the customer who is giving them their paycheck each week.

In 1988, I was flying from Frankfurt to New York on a major European airline. The flight attendant asked me what I would like to drink with dinner and I replied, "Milk." In a very abrupt voice she said, "Milk is for children. What else do you want?" Now I have no idea if this is the airline's policy or if this particular flight attendant was just having a bad day, but it definitely did illustrate a lack of flexibility.

Only a few companies have managed to convey this message to 100% of their employees: do whatever it takes to satisfy the customers' requests. Crystal Cruises, by hiring people with great attitudes toward service, has created a culture of genuine service. You can't be successful if you can't be flexible.

One day at lunch I was ordering a smorgasbord of a sandwich and wanted a few items left off. The waiter very politely said, "You create your own sandwich; we will gladly make it for you." I have eaten away from home an average of 225 days a year for most of my adult life and nobody in the food business has ever given me that option.

Wherever you go on a Crystal ship, you can sense the flexibility. They are there for YOU.

To the thousands and thousands of food establishments who have filed for bankruptcy over the years: Look back at how inflexible you were and how guilty your employees made the customer feel when they dared stray from exactly what was on the menu.

I previously mentioned the book Moments of Truth, by SAS Chairman, Jan Carlzon. In it he vividly points out that each and every employee, when they have a face-to-face encounter with a customer, is truly facing a "moment of truth." And it is these thousands of "moments of truth" every day that ultimately make or break a company.

To face those "moments" most effectively, employees must be given some degree of flexibility. Obviously there have to be some guidelines, but the most important guideline is that the employee can be flexible enough to ensure that the customer receives the best service possible.

Flexibility is very important in dealing with customer complaints. Ritz-Carlton has the philosophy that all corporations should use, and that is "Any employee who receives a guest complaint owns that complaint." In other words, it is their responsibility to get things solved. The company and the employee then have the flexibility to find the best solution for the customer. Policy and procedures manuals should be guidelines for the most part. What makes for a remarkable service experience is when you know the employee went out of their way and on a different path from the norm in order to help you.

Rate your company on its performance in the area of flexibility.

Communication at All Levels

"Don't just watch, but see. Don't just hear, but listen. Don't just talk, but communicate."

The word communication has many meanings. For some it means command of the written word. For others it is the ability to speak thoughtfully and clearly, or being a good listener, or the awareness of good body language. All of these are important, and if a company expects to be successful, they must not only have good communication at all levels, but an ongoing program to teach communication skills to each and every employee.

In the service industry, everyone needs to learn the importance of a smile. A smile is the universal form of communication, and often the only form of communication we have when we are traveling. A friend of mine visited the opening of the Pizza Hut in Russia in 1990. He said that every one of the employees was taught to have this wonderful smile—that people would show up just to be in an environment with a lot of happy people! That Pizza Hut became the number one profit-making center of all the Pizza Huts worldwide at the time.

It is amazing how you never see some people's teeth. These are the same people who wonder why they cannot sell properly and why customers and managers do not respond as favorably as they would like. When you see a photo of them, it looks as if they have just been booked at the local police station. They must be taught the importance of a smile, and how to smile comfortably, if it does not come naturally. Have them look in a mirror, videotape them, or do whatever is possible to ensure that whomever they are interacting with will receive a warm, friendly smile.

You have probably heard some variation of the saying "You have twice as many ears as mouths and should use them in that proportion." Listening skills are very important to effective communication; I believe that one of the courses that should be introduced in school is how to listen. I'm talking about "active" listening—not only hearing and understanding what is said, but showing that you're listening. I am always amazed at how few people in an organization really know how to listen. Yet this is crucial in the service industry, and companies should take the time for training in this area.

After someone has learned how to listen, they can then practice their communication skills verbally. Although fear of public speaking is number one on most people's "fear list," and they can still remember their hearts pounding at 200 beats per minute when called upon in school to speak before their classmates, one of the best gifts an employee can receive is the opportunity to practice these skills. Given the opportunity, training and encouragement, an employee can break down the barrier of insecurity and gain self-confidence in verbal communication. Even if someone does not do a lot of public speaking, they will be more confident in their everyday communications and will be more comfortable speaking in front of others should the situation arise.

Whenever you ask people their preferred method of communication, the majority of people respond that they prefer writing to speaking. Yet, I don't think there is anything we do more poorly in our society today than respond to letters or emails. It is amazing how few people are concerned with replying on time. The best leaders and best corporations have a simple philosophy, which is called "The Sun Down Rule." Reply to all letters and emails in 24 hours and all phone calls before the sun goes down. A successful service company has a philosophy and policy for effective and prompt written communications.

The original Pan American World Airways, perhaps the world's greatest airline ever, closed their doors on December 4th, 1991. Pan Am was made up of the best and the worst. They had some of the brightest minds in the industry, some incredibly dedicated and committed workers, yet the airline's real downfall was the inability to communicate. Even in the '70s and early '80s, I spoke with many brilliant Pan Am people who became frustrated because they could not get a reply from Pan Am's headquarters in New York.

Over the years I traveled to many Pan Am stations, employees shared with me numerous problems that were costing the airline millions of dollars—problems which could be easily rectified by a letter or a phone call. Over a 3-year period I sent 23 personally addressed letters to the office of the president of Pan Am, yet I didn't receive a single response. During the six years researching this book, this was my most frustrating experience, because I loved the history and scope of Pan Am. It is a shame to see such a wonderful institution die out, simply because communication was not a priority, either internally or externally. I don't think I have ever seen a company like Pan Am where there was such a feeling of camaraderie, loyalty and emotional attachment. Even today Pan Am parties draw large numbers to reminisce. Yet many wonderful people were let down by poor communication from senior management.

Finally, I would like to touch upon communication in a company as it relates to evaluation. Many employees are fearful about receiving evaluations. And believe it or not, many leaders are just as uncomfortable giving those evaluations. Here is a simple solution. Ask new employees—and all employees periodically through their career—a very simple question: How would they like to be evaluated? Do they want it to be done in public or in private, in writing or in discussion, in a group or individually? Do they want to receive suggestions and comments as a situation arises? A day later or a week later? If you take 50 employees, you will most likely get 50 different answers. Yet for some reason, leaders tend to want to do evaluations the way they want it done, rather than how the employees want it done. The purpose of an evaluation is to help the employee get to the next level and work on the areas that can help them become a better individual and worker. Do it on their terms and you will see a world of difference.

The best service companies stress effective communication at all levels—with customers, among employees, and between employees and management—and they train their people accordingly.

How does your company rate in these areas of communication?

Thriving on Evaluation

"The trouble with most of us is that we would rather be ruined by praise than saved by criticism."
NORMAN VINCENT PEALE

Any company that hopes to survive long-term must be passionate about reacting to customer feedback. As many corporations have struggled through recessionary times, they were finally forced to really listen to the customer. Guess what happened? They started to realize that customers who complain and are dealt with satisfactorily actually become more loyal in the long run.

The last ten or so years have seen lots of innovations. Corporations are now realizing that what your customer says is not something to be feared. If customers get too easy, service gets sloppy. With evaluation comes the opportunity to make things better. I like the managers who say, "If you don't tell us what is wrong, we don't have a chance to improve."

A word of caution: it is very important that a company not solicit evaluations unless they're prepared to respond.

Sometimes companies are proactive in their evaluation in that they survey the customer in advance. Several hotel companies now send out questionnaires to many of their frequent customers to find out what services and features are important to them when they stay at the hotel on business trips or on pleasure trips. Embassy Suites managers at each property personally survey five customers per day during their stay to hear their thoughts and suggestions. This has greatly enhanced their product, which is already a good one.

But there are always people and enterprises who could not care less about your evaluation. Such was the case in New York when I was at a fast-serve pizza place. I took the first bite and the pizza was cold. The lady behind the counter was scurrying back and forth trying to take care of the lunch crowd. Although she refused to have eye contact with any of her customers, I did manage to call out to her as she was whizzing past that my pizza was cold. Without breaking stride she called back, "No it's not."

One of the advantages of writing a book is that you get a chance to share your pet peeves beyond your local sphere of friends. If there is one thing I would like to eradicate, it is the "police interrogation" on the phone. Here is what I mean. (I am PB.)

PB: "Could I please speak to Mr. Jones?"

Receptionist: "Who's calling?"

PB: "Peter Burwash."

Receptionist: "How do you spell your name?"

PB: "B-u-r-w-a-s-h."

Receptionist: "What company are you with?

PB: "PBI."

Receptionist: "What's the purpose of the call?"

PB: "I am responding to his letter of January 7th."

Receptionist: "I'm sorry, he's not in. Can I take a message?"

During the five years that I have talked to people in researching this book, not one single individual enjoyed the police interrogation, yet it seems that 90% of the corporations in America alone have this style. Why? No one wants it—no one likes it—no one appreciates it. Let's eliminate it. I am including this in the hope that those corporations who "thrive on evaluation" will take this one to heart.

How is your company when it comes to thriving on evaluations?

Summary

Throughout the discussion of the twelve universal principles of great service companies, I hope that you have participated by doing the evaluation yourself and that other employees will share their thoughts and feelings. If your company can score a 9 or 10 out of 10 in each of these categories, you won't have to worry about recessions, depressions, unemployment, shortage of workers or any of the excuses most bankrupt companies use. Whenever a corporation tries to explain why they had to file for bankruptcy, it is interesting to note they never include in their obituary—"We provided bad service."

Part Two

THE 25 UNIVERSAL PRINCIPLES OF GREAT LEADERS

As I mentioned earlier in the book, I originally had no intention to do a section on leadership. However, after the first three years of research, it became evident that one of the problems the service business faces is a lack of good leaders. As I continued to research and interview people in leadership roles, there were common traits that the best leaders exhibited, just as there were common principles for the top service enterprises. Before we look at the universal qualities of great leaders, there are some generalities about leadership that are relevant.

One question that often comes up during presentations on leadership is whether leaders are born or made. Although I have heard one-sided arguments over the years on both sides, my personal feeling is that it's about 50-50. I find it is similar to successful athletes—there are those who are born with a lot of natural talent, and yet there are others who achieve the same success through determination and effort, although they were not born with the same natural ability.

Some people obviously have an innate ability to lead. If you watch a group of children playing, there will inevitably be a natural leader who will take charge of the ongoing events in the sandbox. However, it is important to realize that everyone has to be a leader sometime. Whether you are a parent, a spouse or an employee, part of your day is spent in a leadership role. The great service companies realize this and train each of their employees to be a leader.

What we are going to look at in this section is how our role as a leader transcends our workday and spills into our relationships with friends and family.

Leadership means taking responsibility. Leaders are obligated to provide momentum, to keep people excited and challenged.

Leadership is also a privilege. Certainly we have seen enough examples of world leaders or business leaders who have abused that privilege.

It is very important to realize that, before becoming a great leader, you must learn to be a great follower. The best leaders are those who have served many apprenticeships. Leader truly means ultimate servant. I particularly like the saying, "The measure of a man is not how many servants he has but how many people he serves."

As you read the following chapters, have your pen ready and embark on a self-evaluation process. If you are very strong in a particular area, give yourself a 9 or a 10. Or if very weak, score 1 or 2. You may choose to do this on a separate sheet of paper or use the special chart provided at the end of the book. Subsequently have your spouse, children, employees or co-workers evaluate you. It is always helpful to get another perspective from someone who knows you quite well.

Be honest, this is an opportunity for you to do some sincere self-analysis and embark on the path to improvement.

Before beginning the section on leadership, I feel that it is important that you realize how these 25 qualities came into being. They are a result of 6 years of researching and talking to employees about what THEY wanted in their leader. If you look at most books on leadership, they were written based on interviews with the leaders themselves. I feel that the following 25 qualities are a much more accurate assessment of what a leader is truly all about because they are qualities that employees want, not what the leader feels they want. This is a major difference.

Enthusiastic

"Success is going from failure to failure without a loss of enthusiasm."
SIR WINSTON CHURCHILL

I learned everything I needed to know in the first five minutes of university. In our lives, we get bits of information which turn out to be extremely relevant. For all intents and purposes, the rest of my university career was not necessary.

What happened was very simple. Our first professor, Dr. Kirk Wipper at the University of Toronto

School of Physical and Health Education, wrote in very large, bold letters on the blackboard "ENTHUSIASM IS CONTAGIOUS" and asked all of us to talk about that. After seeing many successful leaders, I realize that Dr. Wipper's opening class was one of the most relevant moments that anyone could have encountered.

Enthusiasm truly makes the difference. There are some people who have a natural vivaciousness about them and you can actually hear them smiling on the phone. They convey they have a grip on life.

As a leader, if you are excited, you draw people like a magnet. People want to keep coming back to spend more time with you. Or they might just want to give you a job. Such was the case with one of the most popular musicians of the 1990s, Garth Brooks.

One day two songwriters, DeWayne Blackwell and Earl "Bud" Lee, went into a shoe store and were helped by Garth Brooks, then just a young clerk. The two songwriters were very impressed with how helpful, friendly and enthusiastic Garth was and they gave him an opportunity to sing some demos. One of the songs they had written was called "Friends in Low Places" and in 1990-91 that song would become the most programmed song of the year, and became the best country single of all time.

When your enthusiasm goes, you're through. Enthusiasm is the foundation of all accomplishments. It is very helpful if you can maintain a childlike enthusiasm throughout your life. If you have ever been with a young child when they see something for the first time, you can hear the excitement and enthusiasm in their voice. Far too often people as they get older become very jaded and lose that level of excitement. Yet enthusiasm is the ingredient that is needed to overcome disappointments.

Tommy Lasorda, the former manager of the Los Angeles Dodgers baseball team, had a very high level of enthusiasm. He said, "The best day of my life was when I managed a winning team, and the second best day of my life was when I managed a losing team."

And enthusiasm isn't just in your voice or your expression, but can also be in your body language. When Helen Keller, who was blind, was introduced to Mark Twain, she said, "I can feel the twinkle of his eye in his handshake."

If we look back and remember what our first day was like in many situations—whether our first date, our first day on a new and challenging job, or our first time visiting a new country—there was always an air of excitement and we were enthusiastic about our new endeavor.

It's easy to be enthusiastic when we are doing something for the first time. The real key to great leadership is to maintain that "first time" enthusiasm when we are doing the same thing over and over again or when we have some trials and tribulations in our life. If you are enthusiastic you will draw people to you like a magnet. Enthusiasm is the electricity of life.

Time to rate yourself on enthusiasm.

Expand Horizons

*"Ships in harbor are safe, but
that's not what ships are built for."*

The best leaders commit themselves to a life of
ongoing personal development. Unfortunately,
with today's emphasis on formal education,
many people believe that graduation is the end
of study. Our formal education program has also
made a mistake in putting so much emphasis on
an individual's earning power once they have
graduated. So often in school, students are told
that if they do well, they will be able to earn.

When I speak at various schools through the year, I tell students that the most important letter in the alphabet is the letter "L" placed in front of "earn". This is what you should do for the first 30 years of your life, and then you will be in a much better position to earn long-term.

With the advent of television, the time that families spend in discussion is now reduced to an average of about 25 minutes per week. The end result is that people have learned to be receptacles rather than innovators. Very few kids today know how to carry on a conversation by way of relevant questions that will help expand their horizons. Rare is the situation today where a teenager asks the first question in a conversation, and the second, and the third and the fourth, genuinely trying to gain further knowledge. In a conversation you can judge a person by the quality of their questions. In fact, one's

progress and success in life is directly proportionate to the number and quality of questions
one asks.

As a parent it's important to make time for
discussion, and to emphasize that there is no
such thing as a dumb question. Noel Irwin-
Hentschel, a very successful business woman
in California, asked her children to clip world
events out of the newspaper and then discuss
them with the rest of the family in the evening.
This is a concept that instills within the young-
sters not only a thirst for learning, but an opportunity to expand their horizons as well.

Over the years in doing media interviews, the
most enjoyable ones were where the interviewer
had the ability to ask thought-provoking questions
and ones that built upon the previous answer.

Good leaders continue to learn, to grow and to develop. Knowledge is the responsibility of the leader. The great ones also give others the opportunity and encouragement to do so.

And to tie it all together—as Aristotle said, "The real purpose of knowledge is one single thought: service." Time to rate yourself.

Avid Readers

"Today a reader, tomorrow a leader."

One of the most important ways of increasing your knowledge and expanding your horizons is through reading. The best leaders love to read. Most subscribe to a lot of different magazines, many of which are outside their area of expertise or current knowledge. They read a lot of biographies or autobiographies about leaders, not only those who succeeded, but also those who failed. They feel a responsibility to read to add to their knowledge and their credibility.

An article in USA Today first pointed out in 1992 that only 4% of the U.S. population bought a book. Unfortunately, the numbers hold true today. Television and computers now monopolize people's time. A long time ago I read that television can take away one's personal creativity. If you are watching television, you are seeing things through the eyes of someone who has produced that program. Yet if you read a book, you can create your own visions. Research shows that the right side of the brain, your creative side, is a whole lot more active when you are reading a book than when watching television. For example, if you are watching television and you see a sailboat gently sailing through the smooth waters of the Pacific Ocean, passing by a tropical island rimmed with sandy beaches, you will simply observe that picture and possibly have a few yearnings to go there. However, as you read that phrase, the right side of your brain is very active conjuring up images.

So many of the world's great leaders, whether business or political, do not watch television. Bill Gates did not own a television for many years. Sir Richard Branson's mom wouldn't allow her son to watch TV when he was younger. She wanted him doing things himself. It paid off, as Sir Richard is one of the most dynamic leaders in the world today.

Very few people would argue that one of the greatest success stories in terms of a turnaround for a country has been Singapore. Although modern Singapore will have some detractors, the majority of people are extremely impressed with Singapore as a success story. Much of this success is attributed to Lee Kwan Yew. Even though he is no longer Prime Minister of Singapore, he still has a significant influence in the country. He is an avid reader and spends a good portion of every morning reading, rather than watching TV.

The late Rod McPhee, former president of Punahou School in Hawaii, one of the most successful educational institutions in America, stressed the value of reading in our education and in our lives. He commented that when he was getting ready to travel he took more time picking out the books he would read on the trip than the clothes he would wear. He also felt that the person who doesn't read is no better than the person who can't read. Many successful business leaders were impacted by Rod's instilling in them a love for reading at a young age.

A concern of McPhee's is that parents do not read to their children enough in the modern era. TV has shortened the attention span of children and the children expect to be entertained all the time. McPhee is a firm believer in the Chinese proverb "Something is learned every time a book is opened."

There is no question that reading stimulates your mind, broadens your knowledge, and enhances your life—and is one of the most important lost arts of our modern society. I agree with the opinion of Thomas Jefferson, who had a voracious appetite for reading. He said, "Great leaders cannot live without books."

The person that won't read has no advantage over the person who can't read. Time to evaluate yourself.

Conscientious Note-Takers

*"Short pen always better
than long memory."*

CONFUCIOUS

As I did research for the book and talked to various employees, I found that one thing that truly irked them was that supervisors or bosses would not write anything down when the employee told them something. Or they would request the employee to write it down and put it on their desk. On the other hand, the best leaders always have a notepad in their shirt pocket or purse and write things down. I also found it interesting in doing the interviews for this book that some of the very successful leaders even took notes during the interview. Writing it down gives you the opportunity to recollect accurately, to remind yourself, and to review things. Writing it down ultimately means remembering it.

Of those I met and interviewed, the winner for effective use of note-taking would have to be Gene Axelrod, founder of the very successful Honolulu Club in Hawaii. For Gene, writing it down means not only remembering, but acting. Gene takes his notepad everywhere, noting ways to improve his business. Ever since I first met Gene I have watched him, keenly observant and jotting down things for his future reference. And he would often implement those new ideas 24 hours later.

When I interviewed employees of Virgin Atlantic Airlines, I heard numerous times from them that their chairman, Richard Branson, writes everything down. Not only did these employees appreciate that he was attentive to their comments and to the details of the business, it instilled confidence in them that things would be taken care of.

We are in an era of major information overload. Anyone who does not have a good system of taking notes is doing a great disservice to themselves, as well as everybody else that they are leading. Whenever you go to a seminar or meeting, always remember that one of the principal reasons for taking notes is for the benefit of all of those people that are NOT in attendance. Good leaders share this information with others on a regular basis. A great leader is never without pen and paper.

How is your note-taking?

Set High
Communication Standards
and Practice Them

*"Communication is the foundation
of all relationships."*

WILL ROGERS

There are many common denominators between the great service companies and the
great leaders.

Communication involves a number of things,
including being able to speak and write well, to

listen attentively, and to exhibit good body language. It is being able to respond to letters and phone calls quickly.

The area we seem to be most deficient in these days is the art of listening. There is a specific reason why we have twice as many ears as mouths—and why our ears are designed never to shut but our mouth is. When we are speaking, we are not learning.

What separates the great leaders from others is that they have truly learned the art of listening. Whether you are a parent, a spouse or a division leader at work, it is important that you have this skill. In fact, one of the most important classes you can enroll in is a class on how to listen. I would love to see a class on listening incorporated into our school system. Not only would it accelerate our learning curve, it would greatly enhance our "success in life" curve. If you think about it, we want students to be good listeners yet not one minute is spent on teaching this skill to the students. We just expect the students to have it. Why don't departments of education set aside the first day of class to spend giving the students some direction?

The following two anecdotes illustrate to me the importance of the proportionate use of mouth and ears.

The first occurred on a flight I had from Washington to Los Angeles. There were two gentlemen sitting behind me, one an American and one from Japan. The American gentleman asked the Japanese gentleman, "Where are you from?" The response was "Tokyo." This question is a fairly common one posed to foreigners in our country and they have learned to recognize it. The American gentleman then proceeded to comment on how many times he had been to Tokyo, how much he liked the city and he went on for 20 minutes in a one-way conversation. During the entire time the Japanese gentleman said only, "Ah, so." Then after the 20 minutes the American turned and asked him a question. Without a beat, the Japanese gentleman politely responded, "So sorry, no speak English." Our American friend excelled in the art of "babbling," but failed in the art of conversation.

The second incident was a meeting I had with the general manager of a resort in California. After the perfunctory, "Hello, how are you doing this morning?" this fellow then embarked on a two-hour one-way conversation. I asked questions the entire time and made sure that they were short questions, because he had the habit of beginning his answer half-way through the question if it was too long. At the end of the two hours we got up, shook hands and I went off to a day of meetings. That evening in the lobby of the hotel I met the executive assistant manager who said to me, "Peter, did you ever impress our general manager. He raved about what a nice guy you were." In the elevator going up to my room I reflected upon how we are perceived when we seldom open our mouth, but rather ask questions and listen with interest. It was a good lesson.

Larry King, the well-known television and radio interviewer, comments, "Nothing I say this day will teach me anything. So if I'm going to learn, I have to do it by listening."

Of course, although listening is essential to good leadership, it is also necessary to communicate. Often when we think of communication, we think only of verbal communication. But good body language is also an integral part of expression. That's another class we should institute in schools. And it should start with a smile. The story of the Pizza Hut in Russia, relayed in Part 1/Chapter 11, exemplified the importance of a smile. In a country which was experiencing hard times, those smiles provided a welcome relief for many people.

In addition to the smile, we must also remember to laugh. It's a shame that children laugh so much and adults laugh so little. Every company or organization should have a laugholigist— someone who makes people laugh. It is good for our health. Every time we laugh, happy hormones are released.

A lost art in communication is the ability to ask questions—questions that keep building upon the information you are receiving in the conversation. A master at this was Rob Thibaut, President of TS Enterprise, a successful restaurant chain. Rob loved to learn, and through his conversations with others and his skill at asking question upon question, he gained an amazing amount of knowledge. As a leader, this ability was also most appreciated by those he worked with. It showed that he was listening and interested, and valued their thoughts and participation.

Albert Einstein once said, "I have no particular talent. I am merely extremely inquisitive."

Good written communication skills are also very important. Written communication by good leaders is clear, effective—and timely.

Somehow or other we have gotten in the habit of not responding to letters, and it seems that we do not take this area of responsibility seriously. Corporate America is terrible at this. The best leaders respond to letters and emails they receive in 24 hours. The master of the 24-hour reply was the late Dick Holtzman Sr., former President of Rockresorts. Dick said he always asked his managers to respond within 24 hours, even if they didn't have the full answer that was needed. They were to tell the person at the very least that they had received the letter and would be getting back to the sender after the matter was reviewed.

Response to telephone calls should be equally prompt, returning phone calls based on what we called earlier "the sundown rule"—to get all phone calls returned before the sun goes down.

Although as kids we often rebelled against our parents' wishes and teachings, I have to look back and say that one of the most valuable lessons my mother taught me was the art of writing thank you notes. From the time I learned to write she insisted that on Christmas Day, all thank you letters had to be completed, responding to those people who had given me gifts before I could go out to play. All of us should carry a little box of thank you notes in our briefcases or have them handy in our desks. Part of good communication is being able to say thank you, whether in person or by letter. Every day of our lives, someone does something nice for us. The world would be a better place if we all learned to be more appreciative of those things—and to express our appreciation. And remember that in today's computer era, a hand-written thank you note is a rarity and will be remembered and in most cases, kept. Whereas, a thank you sent by email is often trashed or deleted right away.

So, how are you when it comes to your communication skills? Do you reply to letters and return your phone calls quickly? How is your smile? Are you a good listener? Remember, good leaders not only ask questions, but they really listen to the answers.

Incredibly Adaptive

"To learn is to change."

Jerry Coffee, who was a prisoner of war for 7½ years in Vietnam, wrote in his book *Beyond Survival*, "The only real security we have is the certainty that we have the equipment to handle whatever happens to us." While it is important to have goals and plans for achieving them, so often circumstances can cause those plans to go astray. Great leaders are confident in their "equipment to handle whatever happens." They are adaptable—able to change or conform to new circumstances without a lot of difficulty.

Leaders are themselves often "change agents," or those who are responsible for altering the course or direction in which we're going. Yet they also must cope with changes that do not occur by choice, but rather are forced upon them by circumstances beyond their control. Whenever you lead people, you must be ready to be adaptable. I have often heard corporate leaders jokingly say that their company would be a great company if it weren't for the people. They are aware of course that their company would be nothing without the people within it, but they are also aware that they must cope with any variety of circumstances which may arise and change people's lives.

Walter Reuther, one of the most respected union leaders of this century, was an individual who loved change and was very adaptable. In fact, his daughter Lisa once recalls walking with him in the Black Forest in Germany. They came to an area where there was no path and he loved it. Great leaders are like that. They love treading down new paths.

People, by their very nature, will force you to be adaptable as a leader. How is your adaptability?

Maximize Time

*"God help me to maximize my
time productively."*
Vietnam POW, Jerry Coffee

Most people invariably think "maximizing time" means working harder or doing more in the time-frame they are at work. However, I am not going to touch that subject in this chapter because there are so many other areas in which we don't maximize time well.

Recently, a studious individual got on the computer and found that in America, if you live to be

72 years of age, you will spend six years of your life standing in line. Wouldn't it make sense to devise a personal plan to do something during those six years of your life? Watch people standing in line. There are only so many positions to stand in, things to glance at or places to put their hands, and then they start the process over again. Instead, whether you are in a customs line at the airport, a bank line or the grocery store, take something along with you—simple paperwork, or a magazine or book you want to read.

There are three other very important areas I would like to discuss with regard to maximizing time. The first revolves around recreation time. If you note, the word recreation can be looked at as re-creation. This is the time when we need to re-create. People who don't take vacations or carve out blocks of time to re-create will inevitably be more moody, more on edge and less emotionally balanced. The mind, in particular, needs a time to re-create. Sitting on a secluded beach with your cell phone and PC is not a smart move; vacations are an opportunity to rejuvenate your spirit. Always remember Rabbi Kuschner's now famous quote: "You'll never see someone on their deathbed saying, 'Gee, I wish I would have spent more time at the office.'"

The second area where we maximize our time poorly is during the work day. We have become so obsessed with trying to pack as much into an 8-hour day as possible that we have eliminated one of the most important parts of a daily routine, namely the "cat nap." Until the industrial revolution, all societies took a cat nap. The largest meal was in the middle of the day, after which was a cat nap. Some societies extended that cat nap into a full length siesta. However, anyone who has experienced a 1-2 hour "nap" in the afternoon may have found it very difficult to get their energy level cranked back up for the rest of the day. A long nap makes us sluggish, but a short 15-20 minute cat nap, or "power nap" as Dr. James Maas, psychology professor at Cornell University calls it, revitalizes us. It has been shown statistically that our work performance will be increased dramatically for the rest of the day after a cat nap. Dr. Maas maintains that the typical executive has a serious dip during the day. Power-napping is designed to overcome drowsiness and restore alertness, although it will not overcome sleep deprivation. He also points out that the power nap is much more effective than drinking coffee to rebuild your alertness level. The body has a physiological need to lie down about eight hours after you wake up in the morning. The best present the corporate world could give to its employees would be to reinstitute the cat nap.

The third area is our "dream time"—a time to reflect, relax, and dream. I have one picture above my desk in the office—a picture of an isolated island in the South Pacific. I go there for 15 minutes every day. Everyone has their dream place, whether it is a deserted island, the top of a mountain, or sitting on the bank of a river. We all need our dream destination where we can go and isolate ourselves from the frenetic energy of this fast-paced world. Our dream destination is becoming more important as the pressure mounts in our cyber-speed telecommunications era. Michael Ledeen, resident scholar for the American Enterprise Institute in Washington, points out that a problem for today's American Presidents is they don't have any "dream time." Every minute of their day is scheduled. This is a major inhibiting factor in their ability to look into the future needs of the country and its people. Every leader should have a little bit of

Steven Spielberg in them who says, "I dream for a living." Remember, "Anyone can dream while they're asleep, but successful people dream while they're awake."

Now I know what is probably going through your mind: "If I take a 15-minute cat nap and 15 minutes of dream time, I'll be in the unemployment line very quickly." However, in dealing with this practically, the ideal situation is to have a boss or leader who realizes the importance of these two endeavors. Or you may have to do it on your own personal time. Regardless of your situation, you should do your best to incorporate them into your daily activities. Maximizing your time, being alert, focused and productive pays big dividends.

How are you doing in this area?

Visionary

*"Good leadership is knowing
how much of the future can
be introduced into the present."*

The future will always belong to those who
see the possibilities long before they become
obvious. They have a vision of something that
could be, and then work to make it a reality.

In the airline industry, the greatest visionary
was Juan Trippe, the founder of Pan American
World Airways. At one time Pan Am was the
benchmark of success in business. It was a true

visionary company, and Juan was the vision behind Pan Am's flights around the world. When
he first decided that he wanted to fly to Asia,
he got out the big circular globe in his office
in New York and rotated the globe so that he
could mark the islands where he could touch
down in traveling from San Francisco to Manila.
There were islands like Hawaii, Wake, Midway,
and Guam—tiny dots in a vast ocean—that
could provide refueling stops. Juan visualized
that this flight could happen; and when the
"China Clipper" finally landed in Manila in the
late '30s, his vision became a reality.

My modern-day visionary award in the business
community definitely goes to Richard Branson.
Although he's got a multitude of companies,
what many people don't realize is that he's had
his share of failures. For Richard Branson, each
day is a series of new visions.

Seeing the possibilities that exist in the future is analogous to the way hockey "superstar" Wayne Gretzky played hockey. As he explains it, "Most players skated to where the puck is. I skated to where it would be." For example, Montgomery Ward began a mail order catalog in 1872. Who would have thought that mail order catalogs would become such an integral part of our lives?

Great leaders think beyond their boundaries. They are never satisfied with their current level of performance. One of the most interesting people I have met in the hospitality industry is Bob Burns, former Chairman of Regent International Hotel Company. One of Bob's main goals was to redesign hotel rooms to best suit the needs of his customers in the most practical way. But he didn't stop there. He constantly traveled the world looking at new facilities and trying to come up with an even better room.

During seminars, people often ask me how they can become more of a visionary and I reply that the first step is to become an avid reader. Reading expands your horizons. As mentioned earlier, readers will tend to be more creative than people who watch television, and being creative is a step toward being a visionary. I urge parents to nurture creativity in their children, and leaders to encourage new ideas from their employees, to help them on their way to becoming visionaries themselves.

There's an irrepressible spirit born into every human being and it takes courage to move forward as a pioneer. Because the future is unknown, we often see it with a tremendous amount of uncertainty. Yet there are great leaders who have had enough visionary skill to anticipate—and therefore have command over—their future.

It is important to realize that not all leaders are instilled with natural visionary capabilities. Keep in mind that President Rutherford Hayes, a former president of the United States, said to Alexander Graham Bell, upon seeing Bell's new invention the telephone, "This is a nice idea, but who would ever want it?"

And sometimes one is forced into being a visionary. Almost everyone who has seen the actor Robin Williams in a movie sits in awe watching his outstanding, creative communications skills. A lot of this was due to the fact that Robin Williams was very lonely as a child and he put together a make-believe world.

How do you score as a visionary?

Secure

*" Great leaders get people to think
more of themselves, not
more of the leader. "*

Good leaders build confidence. They get you
to see that there are no traffic jams in the extra
mile. And in order to build confidence in others, you must yourself be confident and secure.

Secure people encourage others and they enjoy the successes of their friends, family and
employees. They "catch people doing things

right," as Ken Blanchard called it in *The One Minute Manager*. Secure people appreciate the efforts of others and they go about life leaving "sparks of gratitude". Secure people are also able to surround themselves with people more qualified than themselves.

The flip-side of the secure person is the individual who is very insecure. They spend the majority of their time being negative and criticizing. These life losers seem to get a great sense of accomplishment by knocking others. They criticize how you look, what you wear, how you talk, how you act, becoming master critics of everyone but themselves.

If one has watched the daytime talk shows in America recently, one would think we were having a universal nervous breakdown in the country. This "confession obsession" just brings forth into the limelight how much insecurity there is today.

Another form of insecurity is when people become egotistical. Nowhere is this more evident than the self-promotion and self-celebration that takes place in professional football after a touchdown is scored. Instead of doing their little performances for the fans, they should make it a priority to go and express their appreciation for the other ten players who were the real reason they were able to cross the goal line.

Take a look at yourself as a leader. You can score high in the security category if you are the type of individual who not only catches people doing things right, but also expresses an excitement and appreciation for the accomplishments of others.

Hold Up Under Pressure

"Pressure is a privilege. It only comes to those who have earned it."

BILLIE JEAN KING

The above quote by Billie Jean King, former tennis great and one of the founders of the women's professional tennis circuit as we now know it, is my favorite relating to pressure. During a press conference, Billie Jean was asked how she dealt with pressure and this was her response. If you think about it, it is only those who have worked themselves into a position of leadership and responsibility who have the opportunity to deal with the pressure situation when it presents itself.

Personally, I feel the most pressure-filled job in the world is a goaltender in Ice Hockey. The reason is: every time they make a mistake a little red light goes on behind him. Can you imagine if all of us were outfitted with a little red light that would flash on behind us each time we made a mistake? Now that's pressure.

Pressure can also come in the form of criticism. Yet criticism is often the price to pay for being successful. If you don't have critics, you usually aren't having a lot of success. One of the biggest challenges people face in their careers is being able to handle the pressure that comes with success.

Many leaders are faced with very tough situations, balancing the varying pressures of making money for stockholders or being popular with employees, while doing what they believe to be morally right. We have seen this difficulty in politics, where leaders feel the pressure to be popular, trying to be re-elected, instead of just trying to be great leaders.

Great leaders respond well under pressure. They are decisive, thrive on challenges and love competition. A leader who is secure and feels good about himself can stand outside of pressure and do what he believes to be right, rather than what is popular or lucrative.

As a young child playing in the sandbox there wasn't a whole lot of pressure on us. But as our role as a leader increases, it's important not to complain about the pressure, but see it as a responsibility that we have earned.

How do you hold up under pressure?

Self-Discipline

*"Without self-discipline
your life is chaos."*

Good leaders have an exceptional ability to be self-starters. There is a difference between being well-disciplined and being "self" disciplined. Obviously the military needs well-disciplined people, but in the business and family world self-discipline is more important. Self-disciplined people are able to take the initiative and are able to make a commitment to all facets of their lives.

The self-disciplined person is the individual whose feet hit the floor the moment the alarm rings in the morning. They do not push the snooze alarm 4-5 times before finally rolling out of bed. Self-disciplined people have been able to beat the disease of procrastination. They don't have to punch into a clock at work. You can count on self-disciplined people.

If you are a leader looking for future leaders in your company, select those who have a high sense of self-discipline. In the end, these are the people who will really count and make a difference.

How do you score in the area of self-discipline?

Make Lots of Mistakes, But Don't Repeat Them

*"If you are not making mistakes,
you are not making decisions."*

Mistakes are the building blocks, as well as the price you pay, for improvement. Great leaders do not worry about their mistakes—they learn from them. You can win tomorrow, if you know why you lost today.

A few years ago we interviewed young tennis players after they played a match. When we talked to the winners and asked them what they had learned, the response was very short; yet when we talked to the losers, they had lots to say. The lesson is that we learn much more when we lose. The key is to learn from our loss so that we don't repeat the same mistakes. Most of us would learn from our mistakes if we weren't so busy denying that we actually made them.

Whenever I talk about great leaders making lots of mistakes, people immediately say they can score very highly in this area. It is, however, important to note that the great leaders make lots of mistakes only once. There are far too many people who keep repeating the same mistakes.

Great leaders are trailblazers. They are experimenters. They stick their necks out and therefore inevitably make lots of mistakes. People

THE KEY   PART TWO

like this have the courage to take action where others hesitate.

Leaders who succeed in life do not worry about the mistakes they have made. They know that mistakes are going to happen and they are willing to live with the consequences of their decisions. Too much time is wasted by people agonizing over a decision because they're afraid of making mistakes.

Have you made a lot of mistakes lately? Have you made them only once?

13

Steady in Moods

*"One of the key ingredients of
a great leader is consistency."*

Steadiness in their boss or leader probably
meant more to the employees I interviewed
than anything else. They did not like having
a leader whom they could not be comfortable
talking to before he or she had three cups of
coffee in the morning. They shouldn't have to
dread dealing with someone in a bad mood, or
hold back questions or information until someone is in a good mood.

Moodiness truly hurts the atmosphere of a business or of a relationship, as does the loss of temper by a boss or leader. Too often what is said during anger is something we regret when our emotions are calmed down.

Today we have large sections in bookstores on food management, time management and money management, but there's very limited information on mood management. If we can't manage our own moods, how do we expect to be able to lead others properly?

People really appreciate someone whose moods are consistent. This steadiness allows people to keep things in perspective to see what is really important in a given situation. Employees can be comfortable to ask questions, to make mistakes, to learn, to grow.

In talking to centenarians there seems to be one common denominator that stands out above everything else—the fact that they were easygoing and calm. They had learned to accept the cards that life had dealt them.

And to end on a more humorous note: I recently read a great definition of leadership which said, "It's the ability to hide your panic from others."

How about you—do your moods fluctuate?

P.S. Marital Advice Point #1:

Marry a person who is steady in their moods.

Humble

*"People with humility don't think
less of themselves, they just think
of themselves less."*

Sometimes an individual is told that he is very
important—and he unfortunately believes it.
In the last 20 years something drastic has happened with our athletes in Western society.
Because they make a lot of money and are greatly pampered, they tend to develop an amazing
sense of self-importance. This is why so many
athletes have a difficult time transitioning from

154

the illusory world of sports back to real life.

When Jigoro Kano, founder of the art of Judo and highest-ranking Judoist, was old and close to death, he made a request to his students that they bury him in his white belt, the emblem of the beginner.

Leaders who possess humility don't think of themselves as above the crowd, or feel certain things are beneath them. They understand the phrase "There is no such thing as a menial task, only a menial attitude." I witnessed an example of this during a professional tennis tournament in Montreal, watching the late Wilmat Tennyson, then Chairman of the Board of Imasco, one of the largest companies in Canada. He and his company were hosting the tournament, and there was Wilmat at 10 a.m., an hour before the matches were to begin, checking and cleaning the portable toilets. Here was the chairman of a large and successful corporation, so concerned with important details that he didn't care if he had to do the task himself.

Humility is part of the big picture called attitude. Humility is the crown jewel of all qualities of your character. It is your final achievement as a leader. Mahatma Gandhi often spoke of humility and its importance for leaders. One of his most poignant sayings was "The hour of the greatest triumph is the hour of the greatest humility. Humility is truly the ground floor of your life."

How many great hours have you had in your life?

Exemplary

"What you do is so loud I can't hear what you say."

Many leaders forget that they are always "on stage." We should live each day and perform each action as if it will be on CNN that night for the world to watch. Just as kids watch their parents closely and mimic almost every action, so do employees look to their leader to set the example. Exemplar means teacher by example. A good leader is someone whose example sets the pace and creates the appropriate environment. Once a reporter asked baseball great Joe DiMaggio why he gave 100% every day even if the score was lopsided. His reply was "There might be one kid in the stands who has never seen me play before and I want him to see me at my best."

A trustworthy leader is someone who works as hard, or harder, than anyone else. There aren't any office hours for the exemplar. The late Sam Walton of Wal-Mart fame is often cited as a business leader whose employees learned much from his example. His office was simple, he drove a pick-up truck, and he was approachable to his employees and customers. And from his actions they could see his steadfast belief that the customer was truly the most important person in his enterprise. He constantly visited his stores, met his employees and customers, and stayed close to the people who could make or break the business. Sam Walton's down-to-earth style of management was a big factor in Wal-Mart's success.

Good leaders pay as much attention to the last impression as they do to the first impression. Many people run a 95-yard dash and leave a very poor last impression in the last five yards. We spend a lot of time, money and energy on training for the first impression, but hardly anything on the last impression. Many people have burned so many bridges in their lives that there are now very few rivers they can cross.

Being an exemplar also applies to parents raising children. Good character, like good soup, is usually homemade. Children of all ages close their ears to advice and open their eyes to examples. One of the biggest challenges for parents is to have their actions and their words on the same track. It is very difficult for a parent with a bottle of beer in one hand and a cigarette in the other to tell their child not to smoke or drink. Good leaders are true exemplars who don't send out mixed signals.

I find it interesting that most good leaders have heroes or role models themselves. They are still inspired by them, and continue to learn from the actions of their exemplars. Don't underestimate the power of teaching by example.

Try to live your life so that when your children or employees think of fairness and integrity, they think of you. In life it's not so much what you do, but what others do because of you.

How are you in your role as an exemplar?

160

Use Discipline Wisely

"Discipline is the act of teaching the things that are important in life."

In grade 3, a girl named Ann sat in front of me in class. I thought it would be fun to put gum in her hair and watch her silently struggle to get it out. Instead, she screamed out loud and I got caught. The teacher took me behind the black board and strapped 10 times the hand I used to put the gum in Ann's hair. There was no detention—no time out; no conflict resolution class; no trip to the principal—just instant karma. And that was my last indiscretion in class, ever. Yet somewhere in the 1950s and '60s there began a dramatic shift in this concept of discipline. With the liberalization of society, the concept of discipline took on a negative meaning; and in both child-rearing and education it seemed there was an implication that discipline would stifle self-expression or individuality. What people have failed to realize is that without discipline there is chaos. Actually the word discipline comes from the Latin word "disciplina," meaning instruction or training, and it is a positive and necessary thing when used wisely and carefully. The great leaders do not shy away from discipline when it is needed. It is an opportunity to teach someone, and to help them improve. I am not suggesting the reinstatement of the strap, but our disciplinary guidelines of today are so weak that 60% of the kids go into the principal for misbehaving and 65% of the prisoners in American prisons today are routine offenders.

What still hurts many businesses is that there are general managers and supervisors who have a philosophy called "My Way or the Highway." These leaders run their operations by fear and seem to take delight in using firing as a form of discipline. I noted with interest the effect such a new manager had on a hotel that I used to stay at in Singapore. The previous manager smiled, was friendly and really cared about the employees. When you walked into the hotel, all of his employees welcomed you with warm, sincere smiles. His successor, however, seemed to take delight in abusing his employees and instilling fear throughout the ranks. About four months after he took over, walking into the hotel was very much like walking into a morgue. This general manager had killed the spirit of the hotel. It no longer had any heartbeat.

Discipline must be reasonable, not emotional, and balanced by the use of positive reinforcement for good efforts and results. It is also important that after you have disciplined someone, you give them some space and time to work on the areas you talked about. There is an old Indian proverb that says, "Do not criticize someone for being dirty while he is taking a bath." When I interviewed employees, one of the deep concerns they expressed was that they continued to be disciplined "while they were taking a bath." In other words, their boss disciplined them, and they immediately began to work on that area of weakness. However, with no recognition for the improvements they were making or their sincere efforts to improve, the manager would continue to discipline them in that same area.

How do you score in the area of using discipline, wisely and carefully?

Treat Everyone with Equal Respect

"Anyone can be polite to a king, but it takes a gentleman to be polite to a beggar."

Great leaders look at the executive vice president and the janitor as equals. One of the most delightful experiences I ever had while staying at a hotel was at the Sonargaon Hotel in Dhaka, Bangladesh. During my stay there, I thoroughly enjoyed watching then General Manager, Tony Bruggemans, with the employees. Although there were about 700 of them, Tony knew each employee's name—and many Bangladeshis have very difficult names to pronounce. He treated each of them with the utmost respect. In contrast, I have watched other leaders who hardly even smile when they are greeting their subordinates. Yet, when the owner of the company comes in, they have a completely different attitude.

We often treat people according to their rank or title on a business card. You can learn a lot about someone when you see how they treat the lowest person on the totem pole. The owner of a restaurant in Chicago related an amusing story to me, about the varying "importance" of workers. The manager of his restaurant came to him requesting a raise for the waiters and waitresses. The owner replied that he would have to give the raise to the dishwashers as well.

When the manager replied that the waiters and waitresses were more important, the owner suggested they talk further about it the next day.

That evening, just as the first group of customers were finishing eating, the owner sent the dishwashers home. With a second seating coming, you can imagine the chaos in the kitchen. The manager got first-hand experience in seeing that the waiters and waitresses were not more "important" than the dishwashers. Everyone is important and should be seen as such.

In talking to couples who have had their 50th wedding anniversary, there was a common thread of mutual respect and politeness that enabled them to reach this milestone. If couples treat one another the same way they did when they first met for the rest of their life, they will have a long and happy marriage.

I like a quote on this by Booker T. Washington, the most influential black leader and educator of his time in America. He says, "No race can prosper till it learns that there is as much dignity in tilling a field as in writing a poem." The best leaders treat everyone with equal respect. In fact, we could cure our prejudicial problems if we could just transcend the seven layers of skin and look at everyone as valued citizens of the world, rather than a particular race, religion, nationality or position.

How do you score when it comes to treating everyone with equal respect?

Good Teachers

"The best teachers give students an understanding—and time to enjoy it."

Almost all of us had one teacher in school who stood out above the rest. We may not remember what they taught us, but we remember who they were. Good teachers have more than just a great command of their subject. They can get on another person's wavelength and help them to learn and understand the subject. They also give the student time to reinforce what they have learned, as well as time to enjoy it, explore it and make it their own. Poor teachers are those who pile more and more knowledge on top of their students until they finally become overloaded and cannot take in any more information.

Good teachers also place more emphasis on showing than telling. There is a great deal of truth to the phrase "Show me and I will remember. Tell me and I will forget."

The first question every leader should ask the person they are leading is how do they learn. There are three basic modes of learning: by hearing, by watching, and by actually doing. In studying this for over twenty-five years now, the percentages come out roughly as follows: 5% learn by hearing, 15% by watching and copying, and 80% by doing. Yet most training programs by corporations today are taught by video and lecturing.

Perhaps the most important thing to remember in the end, is that great teachers become genuinely excited when the student learns. And the best teachers take enormous delight in actually being surpassed by their students. The job of a teacher is not so much to teach, but to enable learning. One of the biggest mistakes that parents can make is leaving a lot of money to their children as an inheritance. This is not being a good teacher, as it deprives the children of the value of learning how to struggle and overcome obstacles. And the best teachers have meaningful catch phrases or quotes with which the student can connect. Marcus Allen, former NFL football player and Hall of Famer, said his coaches were always negative and his opinion of coaches was not high. As the model leader of a panel that he was on, I asked him the question, "There must have been at least one good coach?" He then admitted that there was only one and explained that that coach always said, "Make sure...make sure you move here...make sure you watch for this, instead of don't move here etc." Good advice for all leaders.

Good leaders, in their teaching, concentrate on personal as well as professional development. Through their information, inspiration and example, they work to develop the potential in each individual. They are not dictators, but cheerleaders who encourage you to be the best you can. In the end, good teaching is really the effective communication between two individuals.

How do you rate yourself as a teacher?

Opportunistic

*"When opportunity knocks, most
people complain about the noise."*

My favorite example of an opportunist is the
late George DeMestral. Not many people recognize his name, but we all use and recognize
the product he created. One day George was
out walking his dog who had gotten quite a
few burrs tangled in his fur. George was faced
with one of those many opportunities that all
of us have in life, yet most of us allow to pass us
by. George had two choices. He could cut out

173

the burrs, throw them in the garbage, curse at the dog and make sure he didn't go down the same path the next time. Or he could look at the burrs and be amazed by how effective they were in gripping to the fur. George took the latter route, viewed the burrs under a microscope and ultimately created Velcro. How many of us would have thrown the burrs in the garbage?

Marriott Corporation is the largest food provider for airlines in the world today, supplying food to over 100 airports. It all began in 1937 with J. Willard Marriott's restaurant near Washington's Hoover Airport. He saw customers come in, buy meals and then go to the airport for their flight. After seeing this, he visited Eastern Air Transport and arranged to deliver pre-packaged meals to them—hence, the beginning of what we now know as in-flight meals.

Almost every situation in life is an opportunity. How we view the situation makes the difference. A number of years ago the leader of a shoe company sent salesman number one over to Africa to explore the market. The salesman called back and said, "There aren't any opportunities over here in Africa because people don't wear shoes." A few months later, shoe salesman number two was sent over and he called back and said, "Unbelievable opportunity here in Africa. No one is wearing any shoes." The key to being an opportunist is to truly view every day as an opportunity and try to seek out that opportunity. It may arise from an individual you meet, an article you read, a movie you see, or something with great potential like George DeMestral's burrs.

The opportunities are there—do you see them?

175

20

Positive

"Most people go through life stepping on flowers while pointing out the weeds."

I have been involved in the interviewing and hiring of people for over 25 years. And as someone who always sees the positive side of things, I was truly convinced I could take a negative person and help them become a positive person. After 25 years of failure, I have now come to realize that these "Yeah, but" individuals need to go down their own track. You know the type I mean. Their response to a cheery "Nice day today" is "Yeah, but it's going to rain."

Great leaders are positive individuals. They don't fault others and are willing to shoulder the blame. They don't complain; they find solutions. You didn't see Edison complain about darkness, Ford lobby against horses, or the Wright Brothers file a class action suit against gravity. They were positive and believed they could find answers.

When the sun comes up each morning, we really only have one major decision to make and that is: are we going to have a good attitude or a bad attitude. What we wear, how we fix our hair, etc. are all minute compared to this one and only major decision. Far too many people go through life standing at the complaint counter.

Also, outstanding leaders do not hold grudges.

There is a relevant phrase we should all keep in our wallet and that is "As long as the past is in conflict with the present, there is no future." As I interviewed employees and leaders, I realized there are many people carrying heavy emotional baggage because of grudges of the past. The best leaders are able to let go of that negativity.

Perhaps the biggest challenge all of us face today is that there's so much negative news it's sometimes tough to keep a positive outlook. It's probably a good idea to incorporate into your regular activities a news fast (no TV, newspaper, etc.). Try it for 24 hours periodically.

One of the greatest coaches in college basketball history was John Wooden. A saying of his was "Don't let what you cannot do interfere with what you can do." He focused this positive mental attitude on the practice floor as well as during the game. He didn't talk about winning but concentrated on intensity, trying hard and doing your best. His positive approach led his teams at UCLA to a record 10 NCAA championships.

Recently Fortune magazine did a survey and found that 94% of the Fortune 500 Leaders attribute their success to a positive mental attitude.

How are you doing when it comes to being positive?

P.S. Marital Advice Point #2:

In addition to marrying an individual who is not moody, it is just as important to find someone who is positive.

Empathetic

*"To understand him, first walk
in the other man's moccasins."*
INDIAN PROVERB

A major problem we face today is that our educational system is cranking out a lot of people
with MBAs who want to start as managers. This
kind of thought process is damaging both to
the young MBAs as well as to the people they
might potentially be leading. It is impossible to
go into a leadership role until you have walked
in another person's "moccasins." This is why I
feel our educational institutions are doing a lot

of harm by not teaching people to become followers first and leaders second. By being a follower first, we are much more equipped to be good leaders when the time comes.

Empathy is one of the keys to successful leadership. One of the greatest gifts we have as human beings is the power to be empathetic. In fact, in many ways I feel empathy is far more important than intelligence. Generally, men have a harder time developing their sense of empathy; but once it's developed, it enables them to be a much stronger leader. It is very difficult to get your troops to follow if you have not been in the trenches yourself. America saw this in the war in Vietnam, where we had a lot of textbook-trained lieutenants trying to come in and lead a bunch of already jungle-wise veteran soldiers.

To be sensitive to others, it is not always necessary to have physically experienced what they have. When we say to someone, "Put yourself in my shoes," we are asking only that they try to better understand our situation. Empathy can come from asking questions, really listening and trying to see and feel what someone else is. Good leaders do this.

Sometimes our empathy for a situation may plant a seed that will enable us to make a major change later on in life. Such was the case with Abraham Lincoln, who at age 21 saw slaves chained and kicked like wild animals in New Orleans. He never forgot that vivid memory and when he became president, slavery was abolished.

When asked what he thought was the most important criteria as a leader, Pat Foley, former president of Hyatt Hotels, quickly responded,

"Empathy." I later interviewed hotelier Bill Rhodes, who had years earlier worked at a Hyatt Hotel in Chicago when Pat Foley was manager there. At that time Bill was working in the laundry room of the hotel. I asked him what he remembers most about Pat Foley. He replied, "Mr. Foley had empathy for what a tough job we had. We worked in a noisy, windowless part of the hotel. Yet Mr. Foley came down every day to see us and talk about baseball games, my first love." This meant so much to him that he still considers Pat Foley the best person he ever worked for.

How is your sensitivity meter?

22

Trustworthy and Trusting

> *"You may not always be called upon
> to be successful, but you will always
> be called upon to be trustworthy."*
>
> MOTHER THERESA

I previously mentioned Motorola, under the leadership of Bob Galvin, winning the Malcolm Baldridge Award for quality and service. Bob, now Chairman of the Executive Committee of Motorola, spoke to me with great conviction on the value of trust. Bob feels that trust is the strongest motivator. His basic philosophy has been: "If you trust me, I cannot let you down." A customer will buy from a company it trusts, and a company has the responsibility not to let the customer down. So it is with leaders. A leader must have a consistent value system. You will follow someone you can trust, and a true leader honors that trust.

Values were once instilled through the extended family. However, factors such as the breakdown of the family and the inability of the business or political world to provide exemplary leaders with sound value structures have resulted in a very distrusting society. As well, consumerism has achieved a dominance over our value systems. What values do the commercials on television espouse?

In many ways it was wonderful to see what happened in the '80's and '90's. There were so many unethical decisions made by our leaders, both in politics and in business, that ethics were forced to the forefront of people's minds. Suddenly there was a lot to be said for the power of ethical management. Things are a lot more transparent these days with the ever increasing volume of press people, so untrustworthy people will eventually be "ousted" much sooner than in the past.

Still, to be truly effective, trust must be a two-way street. As Bob Galvin adds, "Leaders must trust and accept the people they lead. And such acceptance requires tolerance of imperfection. Anybody can lead perfect people." The basic philosophy of "If you trust me, I cannot let you down," works both ways. People will do their best to live up to your trust in them.

I have known Issy Sharp, owner of Four Seasons Hotels, for many years, and have admired his consistent value structure. The son of a Polish immigrant to Canada, he speaks of the values he saw in his family and in the hard-working immigrant construction workers who used to work with his father. "You never had to oversee a man's work because he was devoted to his job, working sun-up to sunset and innately courteous. They had respect for one another. I grew up doing what they did. You count on each other, rely on each other. That's what we do in Four Seasons today."

Being trustworthy is the single most important contributor to the maintenance of human relationships. How do you rate, both in being a trustworthy person and in trusting others?

23

Have a Spiritual Foundation

"Spirituality is the fountainhead of all religion, values, ethics, and moral principles."

Modern education is sharpening the brain, but we're neglecting the heart. Education of the heart is so important to our continued development as a human being.

The more interviews I had with people, the more I realized that faith was a very important part of their daily lives. It is important here to separate spiritual foundation from religious foundation. Spiritual foundations heal wounds and make us better people. Religion, on the other hand, so often seems to instigate violence rather than eliminate it. Spirituality is the opposite of materialism and includes things you cannot place in your hand, like love, tenderness, caring, understanding, thoughtfulness, dedication, commitment, etc. It is these spiritual foundations in life that also enable us to see ourselves as vulnerable and to feel there is a higher being or power.

Former President F. W. DeKlerk of South Africa, who helped to engineer the abolishment of apartheid in his country, received about 15 death threats a day during the transition period. When I asked him how he dealt with this incredible pressure, he pointed to the sky and said, "My vertical relationship with that gentleman."

I was reminded of his statement while watching a television interview with an American soldier returning from the Gulf War. The interviewer asked what he had learned over there. Sgt. Bobby Nichols uttered that famous phrase, "There are no atheists in bunkers." Great leaders also realize their own personal vulnerability, and a belief in a higher power is a common factor among them.

How do you rate with your spiritual foundation?

Committed

*"I cannot imagine a person becoming
a success who doesn't give this
game of life everything he's got. "*
WALTER CRONKITE

To commit to something is to give it all you've got. Or as Abraham Lincoln expressed his commitment to life: "I do the very best I know how—the very best I can; and I mean to keep on doing so until the end."

I like the story of Bill Toomey's commitment to winning the Olympic Decathlon. In 1964, at age 25, Bill was competing in the Olympic Trials for the Decathlon, the most grueling event of the Olympics. The top three competitors from the trials would qualify for the Olympics, and Bill finished fourth. The next day he was out running around the track. Some of the people who had watched him on the previous day said, "Mr. Toomey, why are you training—you lost." His response was "I am training for the 1968 Olympics." And in 1968 in Mexico City, it was Bill Toomey who had the gold medal placed around his neck.

A commitment is like a pledge to something or someone. For some reason the word commitment has waned greatly in its meaning the last few decades. People change jobs, wives and husbands like they change tires. We are in an advertising era where a lot of promises are made but few commitments are fulfilled. It is not uncommon for people to cancel meetings, to be late and have very little concern with details.

The best leaders are committed—to their principles, to their goals, and to the people they are leading. When you are with a great leader you sense their incredible commitment. In business, as in any relationship, the best leaders know that commitment is a two-way street. Employees will not have any sense of confidence or loyalty to a company whose commitment to them does not extend beyond the bottom line. All you have to do is look at the business section of the newspapers and see how many people are being laid off. What kind of commitment is that? Companies and leaders want you to be committed to them, but when times get rough they feel virtually no commitment to the employee and hand them their termination papers.

How is your personal commitment?

Persevering

*"Get a good idea and stay with it.
Dog it, and work at it until
it's done, and done right."*

WALT DISNEY

If you look at the successful leaders and people who have really made accomplishments in their lives, you will see that they had an undeviating belief in themselves—failed, and yet carried on. Thomas Edison had 1,350 unsuccessful attempts at creating the light bulb and yet persevered. As Albert Einstein said, "I think and think for months and years. Ninety-nine times, the conclusion is false. The hundredth time I am right."

Federal Express is one of the truly great business success stories of our era. Its founder, Fred Smith, received a C in his economics class for the paper which outlined the idea for an overnight delivery service. His professor said it was okay but it wouldn't work. Great leaders believe in themselves and their dream, even when others say it cannot be done. They have the self-confidence and the vision to make it a reality. And they don't give up.

So many people never run far enough on their first wind to find out that they've actually got a second wind. We are made to persevere; that's how we find out who we really are. I once opened a fortune cookie and inside it was a quote which said, "Perseverance is genius in disguise." In the end, success is determined by your will to continue, not by your ability. So often success is really a lousy teacher. One of the key secrets to success is perseverance. It's being able to withstand massive disappointments, massive frustration and massive rejection. Every great leader I've talked to went through all three of these.

In 1979, when Peter Ueberroth was selected to head up the 1984 Olympics in Los Angeles, there was no question that he would have to persevere. Peter did not have the luxury of the financial backing of a government as the previous Olympics had and he was going to have to do it as a commercial venture. Peter was setting out to do something that no one else had ever accomplished before with the Olympics, and he did not have a lot of assets to begin the preparation. He had his own experience and ideas,

a brilliant colleague working with him named
Dick Sargent, a secretary and $100 in the bank.
Yet on the closing day of the 1984 Olympics,
Peter Ueberroth got a standing ovation from
the 80,000 people from whom he had extract-
ed money to purchase their very expensive
tickets for these ceremonies. Peter Ueberroth
persevered.

How are you in the area of perseverance?

Conclusion

Now I urge you to persevere in your continuing development as a leader. Look over how you score in these 25 qualities of the best leaders, and begin working on those areas that need improvement. Keep a realistic perspective, remembering that even the outstanding leaders wouldn't score a 9 or 10 in every category. But remember, too, that developing as a better leader will enhance both your business and personal life, as well as the lives of those you lead.

And as each of us strives to be a better leader, so must companies strive to be better than they were last week. Great leaders and great companies are never satisfied with status quo. They deeply care about improving. It's when they stop caring that they are finished. Companies that are committed to, and truly care about, serving their employees and their customers will be around a long time. When you walk in their doors, you sense that commitment. Great leadership is not what happens when you're around, it's what happens when you're not there.

The 25 Universal Qualities of Great Leaders
Self-Evaluation

By Peter Burwash

Now is the time to get your pen ready and embark on a self-evaluation process. The grading scale is from 1 to 10. If you are very strong in a particular area, give yourself a 9 or a 10. Or if very weak, score a 1 or 2. You may also choose to have your spouse, children, employees or co-workers evaluate you. It is always helpful to get another perspective from someone who knows you quite well.

Be Honest. This is an opportunity for you to do some sincere self-analysis and embark on the path of improvement.

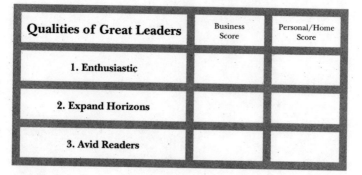

Qualities of Great Leaders	Business Score	Personal/Home Score
1. Enthusiastic		
2. Expand Horizons		
3. Avid Readers		

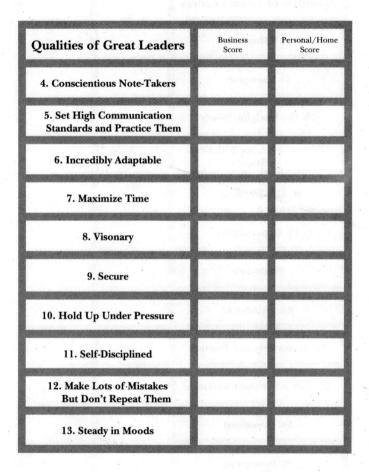

Qualities of Great Leaders	Business Score	Personal/Home Score
4. Conscientious Note-Takers		
5. Set High Communication Standards and Practice Them		
6. Incredibly Adaptable		
7. Maximize Time		
8. Visonary		
9. Secure		
10. Hold Up Under Pressure		
11. Self-Disciplined		
12. Make Lots of Mistakes But Don't Repeat Them		
13. Steady in Moods		

Qualities of Great Leaders	Business Score	Personal/Home Score
14. Humble		
15. Exemplary		
16. Use Discipline Wisely		
17. Treat Everyone With Equal Respect		
18. Good Teachers		
19. Opportunistic		
20. Positive		
21. Empathetic		
22. Trustworthy and Trusting		
23. Have a Spiritual Foundation		
24. Committed		
25. Persevering		

About the Author

Peter Burwash first became prominent in the 1970's as a young professional on the international tennis circuit and soon became well known for his fierce determination, all-out performance and passion for the game.

Peter is now recognized as one of the top tennis coaches in the world, having coached in 134 countries on 5 continents. Peter won 19 international singles and doubles titles and became a Canadian champion and Davis Cup player during his years playing the international circuit. He shares his tennis knowledge with a nationwide audience on CBS radio, as an instruction editor for *Tennis Magazine*, and as a television commentator and analyst. *Tennis Industry Magazine* recognized Peter as "one of the most influential tennis teachers of the past two decades."

As a best-selling author, his book *Tennis for Life* was translated into several languages, revolutionizing the game of tennis around the world. A second book, *Total Tennis*, soon followed, as did award-winning instructional videos, which many consider a "must buy" for any tennis library.

This, his fifth and most recent book, *The Key to Great Leadership—Rediscovering the Principles of Outstanding Leadership*, is a compilation of Peter's research and life experiences, explaining why everyone should consider himself/herself a leader. It provides an opportunity to evaluate one's leadership skills and offers suggestions on how one can be a more effective leader.

In 1975, Peter founded Peter Burwash International (PBI), the world's largest and most successful international tennis management firm. PBI's 110 tennis professionals coach in over 65 of the finest tennis/resort destinations in 34 countries around the world. Listed as "one of the ten best-managed companies in America," Dr. James O'Toole, in his book *Vanguard Management*, stated that PBI "may well be a forerunner of a class of entirely new service organizations."

Traveling over 10 million miles in the last 25 years has not slowed down the man who previously recorded the highest fitness index of any Canadian athlete. Peter is sought after internationally as a speaker and gives over 100 speeches and seminars each year on a variety of topics, ranging from health and fitness to service and leadership.

For more information on PBI or Peter Burwash's
availability as a speaker, please contact:

Peter Burwash International (PBI)
4200 Research Forest Dr.
Ste 250
The Woodlands TX 77381
281 363 4707

PETER BURWASH

LIFE ENRICHMENT LIBRARY

If you liked this book by Peter Burwash you may be interested in the others in his Life Enrichment Library. Please take a look at Peter's four other titles on the following pages and use the ordering information at the back of the book to purchase further copies.

Special prices are available for bulk orders.